MYSTERIES
EXPLORED

The Search for Human Origins, UFOs, and Religious Beginnings

Jack Barranger
Paul Tice

Published 2000
The Book Tree
Escondido, CA

MYSTERIES EXPLORED:
The Search for Human Origins, UFOs, and Religious Beginnings

ISBN 1-58509-101-4

©2000

THE BOOK TREE

THE LEGACY OF ZECHARIASITCHIN
By Jack Barranger
Edited by Paul Tice
© 1996, 2000 Jack Barranger

THE FIRST DRAGON
By Paul Tice
© 1994, 2000 Paul Tice

PAST SHOCK
By Jack Barranger
© 1998, 2000 Jack Barranger

UFOs: FROM EARTH OR OUTER SPACE?
© 1996, 2000 Paul Tice

IS RELIGION HARMFUL? and A CALLFOR HERESY
© 1994, 2000 Jack Barranger

PROMETHEAN FIRE, PLEAIDIAN POOP and INTRUSIONS Newsletters
© 1994, 2000 Jack Barranger

Layout and Design by Tédd St. Rain

Printed on Acid-Free Paper

Published by
The Book Tree
Post Office Box 724
Escondido, CA 92033

We provide fascinating and educational products to help awaken the public to new ideas and information that would not be available otherwise. We carry over 1100 Books, Booklets, Audio, Video, and other products on Alchemy, Alternative Medicine, Ancient America, Ancient Astronauts, Ancient Civilizations, Ancient Mysteries, Ancient Religion and Worship, Angels, Anthropology, Anti-Gravity, Archaeology, Area 51, Assyria, Astrology, Atlantis, Babylonia, Townsend Brown, Christianity, Cold Fusion, Colloidal Silver, Comparative Religions, Crop Circles, The Dead Sea Scrolls, Early History, Electromagnetics, Electro-Gravity, Egypt, Electromagnetic Smog, Michael Faraday, Fatima, The Fed, Fluoride, Free Energy, Freemasonry, Global Manipulation, The Gnostics, God, Gravity, The Great Pyramid, Gyroscopic Anti-Gravity, Healing Electromagnetics, Health Issues, Hinduism, HIV, Human Origins, Jehovah, Jesus, Jordan Maxwell, John Keely, Lemuria, Lost Cities, Lost Continents, Magick, Masonry, Mercury Poisoning, Metaphysics, Mythology, Occultism, Paganism, Pesticide Pollution, Personal Growth, The Philadelphia Experiement, Philosophy, Powerlines, Prophecy, Psychic Research, Pyramids, Rare Books, Religion, Religious Controversy, Roswell, Walter Russell, Scalar Waves, SDI, John Searle, Secret Societies, Sex Worship, Sitchin Studies, Smart Cards, Joseph Smith, Solar Power, Sovereignty, Space Travel, Spirituality, Stonehenge, Sumeria, Sun Myths, Symbolism, Tachyon Fields, Tesla, Theology, Time Travel, The Treasury, UFOs, Underground Bases, World Control, The World Grid, Zero Point Energy, and much more. Call **1 (800) 700-TREE** for our *FREEBOOK TREECATALOG* or visit our website at www.the-booktree.com for more information.

CONTENTS

CHAPTER ONE

THE LEGACY OF ZECHARIA SITCHIN

JACK BARRANGER

In 1976 Zecharia Sitchin published a book which would be one of the seeds spawning a revolution in the way humans would look at their own past. This book, *The 12th Planet*, would challenge much of our consensus reality about what is myth and what is actually history.

With 8 books to his credit Sitchin has in those 25 or so years since *The 12th Planet*, moved from obscure scholar to a lecturer who is in great demand. He is a mild-mannered man whose style is more academic than flamboyant. Yet what he writes about is capable of shattering the foundations of our collective belief systems. Sitchin operates from a highly revolutionary thesis: what you thought was mythology is actually history in many cases – all those gods mentioned in myth after myth were real, and they made quite an impact on the emerging human race.

My own introduction to Sitchin came when I thought I had picked up a "safe" historical book called *The Stairway to Heaven*. I thought that I was going to read more deeply into one of my favorite mythological writings: *The Epic of Gilgamesh*. However, 60 pages into this work I read the following:

> Because the Anunnaki (the so-called gods of mythology) were close to revolt, they made a decision to create a race of beings which would do the difficult work in the mines. This slave race turned out to be the human race.

That rocked me. Not because it was absurd, but instead because it explained what I had been experiencing with many of the 400 interviews I had been conducting for my previous book *Knowing When to Quit*. I had sensed an inability by these people to pursue and embrace what they *really* wanted to do with their lives. I found many who appeared to be stuck in a slave mentality. Their work was more of an obligation than fulfillment. They expected to serve and – despite misery in their work – found it very hard to break free and search for something better.

Could Zecharia Sitchin be on to something? Could his research possibly explain what I saw as a "slave chip" mentality? Is it possible that many people continue to lead highly limited lives because thousands of years ago they were programmed to be slaves?

I began reading other books of his like *The 12th Planet* and *The Wars of Gods and Men* to see if he could offer further insights. I was not disappointed. In his 8 highly researched books with impeccable academic documentation, Sitchin has advanced the thesis that what we have previously considered mythology may actually be history.

Slightly more than 100 years ago, Hermann Schliemann stunned the academic world by providing evidence that the Trojan War actually happened. In the 1960's an American group of explorers used Homer's *Odyssey* as a guidebook and found that they were able to follow the oceanic currents as described in the *Odyssey* and land exactly where the book stated that Odysseus landed. These

The third of the Sumerian Seven Tablets of Creation, that predates the Bible by thousands of years.

and other ventures began putting a crack in the consensus reality that mythology was simply "myth."

As an authority on ancient history, and one of only 200 scholars who can read and interpret the Sumerian language (in addition to Hebrew), Zecharia Sitchin is uniquely qualified to address this kind of issue. As both a scholar and an archaeologist, he is highly respected in academic circles. His revolutionary first book, *The 12th Planet*, came out in 1976 and was read mainly by scholars and lay people willing to embrace the thesis that the Hebrew, Greek, Sumerian, and Babylonian myths were not simply inventions of emerging cultures – but were instead historical accounts.

> There were no more local deities. They were gods – indeed, international gods. Some of them were active and present on Earth even before there were men upon Earth. Indeed, the very existence of Man was deemed to have been the result of a deliberate creative enterprise on the part of the gods.

Sitchin, *The 12th Planet*

This idea is not exactly new. Some archaeologists began exploring this theory in the late 19th century. However, it was not until the late 1960's and into the 1970's that Erich von Daniken with *Chariots of the Gods* and other spin-off books successfully brought the ancient astronaut theory into the mainstream. The idea mainly stated that astronauts from another planet or star system visited Earth and significantly impacted the advancement of the human race. However, von Daniken hurt his credibility by seeing examples of spaceships and astronauts in space gear in far too many ancient carvings and pictures. This – and a lack of readiness of Americans to consider this possibility – caused von Daniken to fall from grace.

After the publication of Sitchin's 1976 *The 12th Planet*, more than 10 years passed before its ideas began spawning a revolution in human thought. This was a far more scholarly work than von Daniken's. One basis for Sitchin's work is that a large inhabited planet in our solar system circles the sun in an extreme ellipsis. He did not make this up – it is recorded in ancient texts like the Sumerian *Karsag Epics* and the *Atra Hasis* (a book which most scholars and theologians admit was the foundation for the first six chapters of Genesis). The ancient Sumerians called this planet Niburu. According to these epics, every 3600 years the planet would enter the circumference of our solar system. As the planet approached, highly advanced beings would leave Niburu and come to Earth to colonize it.

Babylonian cylinder seal depicting the creation of mankind. The tree of life is flanked by modern man on the left and the creator god (Enki) on the right. Note the symbolism of the serpent on the left.

For those who struggle with this as I did, about 20 years ago astronomers at UCLA determined that a large planet is circling the sun in *extreme* ellipsis. They were able to determine this by the gravitational anomalies recorded in the circling of the other eight planets. Could this be the Niburu of the supposedly mythological texts? If the reality of this planet turns out to be the truth, then could the fact that this planet was inhabited also be a reality? If this newly discovered planet is indeed inhabited, could its inhabitants be the creators of the human race?

That is a question which many scientists are willing to consider. Once a week, 150 top scientists meet on-line (conferencing by computer modems) to share their latest insights and discoveries which support what they refer to as *The Nefilim Thesis* – the idea that advanced beings created humanity.

The word *Nefilim* is used in Genesis 6:4.

> There were giants in the earth in those days; and also after that, when the sons of God came in unto the daughters of men, and they bare children to them, . . .
>
> *King James Bible*

Sitchin makes it clear in all his books that "giants" is a mistranslation – that the word Nefilim actually means "those who came down from the sky." That is how the word is translated in the *Atra Hasis* (which the Hebrews drew on for the first 6 chapters of Genesis).

Some other questions from our ancient past continue to haunt us – the largest of these being the "missing link" theory in evolution. Despite Darwin and all who have followed, no one has been able to explain how Neanderthal man advanced so quickly to Cro-Magnon man. Considering how slowly Neanderthal man was advancing, the very quick evolutionary leap to Cro-Magnon man was highly unlikely. Science now shows convincing evidence of both Cro-Magnon and Neanderthals living, for a while, during the same time period! It only makes sense. Should the "experiment" go wrong, an advanced race would not want to eradicate the original race too quickly. Even so, Homo Neanderthalis was totally destroyed within two thousand years after the introduction of Cro-Magnon man – something considered "naturally impossible" based on the long, slow process of evolution. What really happened here?

Zecharia Sitchin does not believe that Cro-Magnon man was solely a product of evolution, but of genetic engineering. His indefatigable research has led him to this conclusion:

> Here then is the answer to the puzzle: the Nefilim did not "create" Man out of nothing; rather they took an existing creature and manipulated it, to "bind upon it" the "image of the gods."
>
> Sitchin, *The 12th Planet*

"What!" say the skeptical. "Not even von Daniken went that far!" Actually, von Daniken did go that far, but America was no longer listening. Despite increased research skills and more credible support, 7 more recent books of von Daniken were not able to find a publisher in America for about 20 years (unlike a more open-minded Europe). A couple have since entered the market, but most remain unavailable.

Sitchin's first book, *The 12th Planet*, had what von Daniken's early books lacked: impeccable scholarship. From his translation of the *Atra Hasis*

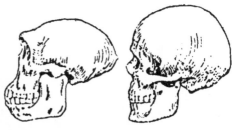

Homo erectus *(Neanderthal Man) at left* compared to **Homo sapiens** *(modern man) at right.*

and recently discovered tablets of *The Epic of Gilgamesh*, Sitchin relates how the Anunnaki were mining on planet Earth and the leaders realized they were on the brink of mutiny. As written by the humans, the stories told of the Anunnaki's increasing problem:

> When the gods, like men bore the work and suffered the toil, the toil
> of the gods was great, the work was heavy, and the distress was much.
>
> *Atra Hasis*

The *Atra Hasis* relates in vivid detail how the main leaders of the Anunnaki debated and determined how they would solve this problem. They were far from home and realized that harsh disciplinary measures would be counterproductive. Finally, they agreed on a solution:

> Let a Lulu (primitive worker) be created
> Let him bear the yoke
> Let him carry the toil of the gods.

From this ancient work, used by the Hebrews for Genesis, comes a tale of how the ancient gods saw a potential problem and then solved it by creating a new species – a feat of genetic engineering. If the Hebrews did indeed take material from the *Atra Hasis* and place it into the first chapters of Genesis, why did they fail to include something this important?

How interesting that people will say it is true if it comes from the Bible, yet will balk at the idea of advanced beings inhabiting the planet in other areas not mentioned in the Bible. We teach our children that Jehovah was real but that the Greek god Zeus was not. For centuries we believed that Moses parted the Red Sea based on just a few Biblical verses, yet until recently we believed that the now proven ten year Trojan War was simply myth. Into the fray of this dichotomy comes Zecharia Sitchin who claims that not only were Zeus and Jehovah real, but they were most likely the same entity. In fact, he takes this idea one step further by claiming that Enlil, one of the main characters of the Sumerian *Atra Hasis*, may have been the foundation for both Zeus and Jehovah.

The subtitle of the *Atra Hasis* is *The Babylonian Story of the Flood*. Sitchin found some interesting parallels in this version of the flood and the Biblical account. In the *Atra Hasis* Enlil declares that he has had enough of this newly created human race. They complain, they rebel, and they make so much noise that he can't sleep at night.

> The god Enlil said to the other gods:
> "Oppressive have become the pronouncements of
> mankind. Their conjugations deprive me of sleep."

His solution: get rid of them. His method: take advantage of an oncoming natural disaster.

However, Enlil has a brother Enki who is *relatively* more compassionate. He goes to the human Utnapishtim and tells him to build a boat which would survive a large flood. Enki suggests to him that he will know the flood is coming when he sees their "sky vehicles" departing (for some reason, the Hebrews decided not to put that small part in Genesis).

The *Atra Hasis* has far greater detail and description of the flood. It tells of Enki, Enlil, and the other gods (the Anunnaki) hovering high above, watching the encroaching flood destroy their human creations. Many of them weep and wonder if they have done the right thing. They watch in horror as millions drown. The *Atra Hasis* goes on to tell how Enki reveals that he has saved Utnapishtim and some of his followers. Enlil is at first enraged, but then is consoled by the fact that some of their creations will actually survive.

Is Zecharia Sitchin starting a revolution? Yes, because he is introducing academically solid evidence that highly advanced beings were here in the flesh over

4000 years ago. He is compounding that revolution by offering solid written evidence – some of it discovered in the last 25 years – that we as humans were created as a work force to fulfill the will of the gods. Backed by evidence from *The Epic of Gilgamesh*, the *Karsag Epics*, and the *Atra Hasis*, we are able to see with a much greater depth what happened during the time that these advanced beings were here.

Much of this is not pretty. Relegating this to the realm of myth would ease the pain. However, Sitchin claims that we must boldly look at our past if we are going to advance as humans. We were programmed to be slaves. Sitchin and his contemporaries suggest that this programming remains with us today (Neil Freer covers this aspect very effectively in his books *Breaking the Godspell* and *God Games*).

One area where Sitchin's schol-

Enki as the Water God, here shown with streams of water with fish flowing from his shoulders. Enki is often represented by the fish-tailed goat or ibex, which combines the two symbols sacred to him.

arship takes a Biblical area to a new level is in the story of the Tower of Babel. The Biblical account, according to the Hebrews, gives the impression that a group of humans were building this tower so they could get closer to the heavens. Sitchin, after many years of probing into the Hebrew and Sumerian languages, feels that the Genesis account doesn't give the full story. A clearer understanding of the Tower of Babel might lie in the more descriptive *Atra Hasis*.

According to the *Atra Hasis*, the humans were not building a tower. They were actually building a rocket ship. Because the Anunnaki feared these newly created beings might actually get off the planet and return to Niburu, the Anunnaki took drastic measures:

> Come, let us go down and confound their language, that they might not understand one another's speech.

Genesis 11:7

Yes, this last example is from the Bible, and this is the main source for Sitchin's claim. He centers his revolutionary thesis around the Hebrew word "shem," which most Bible scholars believe to be the word for tower. However, Sitchin – because of his Sumerian studies and references made to this event in the *Atra Hasis* – *believes that the word "shem" actually means "rocket launching place."*

The *Atra Hasis* suggests that the first human creations were frighteningly intelligent. They balked at the idea of menial work. They questioned the Anunnaki's claim that they were gods. Deceiving these newly created humans was very difficult. The thrust of the Bible suggests that man was like this because he was flawed and wicked. However, the *Atra Hasis* suggests that man was like this because he was highly perceptive and immensely intelligent.

As strange as this might appear, this is not a new idea – nor is it an idea linked strictly to the history of the Middle East. An eerie parallel is found in the Maya sacred book *The Popul Vuh*. After creating a new species, these gods *also* became concerned:

We have already tried with our first creations, our first creatures, but we could not make them praise and venerate us. So let us try to make obedient, respectful beings who will nourish and sustain us.

The Popul Vuh

Halfway around the world, another group of gods were becoming distressed with what they had created. Can we simply write this off as mythology? Could it be that we humans were far more intelligent than expected? Is it possible we were far too intelligent for our own good?

. . . they saw and instantly they could see far, they succeeded in seeing, they succeeded in knowing all there is in the world. When they looked, they instantly saw all around them, and they contemplated in turn the arch of heaven and the round face of the earth.

The Popul Vuh

Could these newly created humans have been so intelligent that they could know more than the Anunnaki had planned for them to know? Could these newly created beings have been so intelligent that they could build a spaceship that would lift them free of their toil?

The Popul Vuh tells of six different creations being necessary before they created a human that would serve and venerate them. It finally claims, "Their eyes were covered and they could see only that which was close . . ." The Bible claims that we had our language confounded and that we were ". . . scattered abroad upon the face of the Earth."

Of course, it is very simple to claim that Sitchin is a misguided scholar and relegate him to the same niche as Erich von Daniken. However, as von Daniken had some good evidence to support his theories, Sitchin has a greater wealth of excellent evidence to more fully support his own. If Erich von Daniken started the fire, Zecharia Sitchin has added fuel and is fanning the flames. Archeological evidence has been and is being discovered which lends credence to the thesis that ancient astronauts were indeed here approximately four to six thousand years ago.

Sitchin quietly adds evidence to this thesis with each new book. His eight books (as of this writing) show an indefatigable scholarship centered strongly in his own personal integrity. Like the diminishing breed of journalist who will not use material until it is solidly confirmed, Sitchin will put nothing in any of his books until he has researched the material thoroughly and verified his findings with support from many sources. Considering the revolutionary nature of Sitchin's writings, one wonders what he has discovered (but not revealed) in which he is still searching for more confirmation.

One gets a hint of this in his 1990 book *Genesis Revisited*. There, the academic scholar leapt into a new realm and claimed that not only had humanity's creators been the Anunnaki of the past, but that those same Anunnaki were on their way back. The safe, staid Sitchin was now claiming that these "creators" would return and expect us to be their slaves once again.

A 1953 government report claims that 90% of humanity would worship these beings. Having interviewed over 40 abductees for articles about alien abductions, I confess to wondering if a link doesn't exist between current UFO activity and the possibility of a "return of the gods."

Sitchin has not disappointed me in stating that:

UFO sightings and/or abduction reports describe the occupants of those vehicles as humanoid, but not exactly human . . . Exactly such beings were depicted in antiquity . . . humanoids sent ahead to perform special tasks.

Sitchin, *International UFO Library,* April/May 1994

In Sitchin's recent works, he speaks a bit more directly on the imminent return of the Anunnaki. He breaks free of focusing mainly on the past and suggests what we can possibly expect in our future. Focusing on recent Mars discoveries and the failed mission of the Mars observer, Sitchin addresses the present:

> As I brought out in *Genesis Revisited* in 1990, Soviet mission controllers interpreted the spacecraft's signals as indicating that the vehicle suddenly went into a spin as if it was hit by something. . . . I suggested that the loss of Phobos 2 was not an accident but an incident – the deliberate shooting down of a spacecraft from Earth by "someone" on Mars who does not wish to be disturbed . . .

> Sitchin, *International UFO Library*, April/May 1994

Time and time again, up to the year 2000, we have mysteriously continued to lose most of our Martian probes due to one "accident" or another. Are these really accidents? How often must this happen before we begin to realize that this may be more than just "bad luck," or the stupidity of NASA for mistakenly using the metric system instead of feet and inches (of all things), in their billion-dollar mathematical calculations?

As I continue to give lectures and radio interviews on my book *Knowing When to Quit*, I sense that something has to be responsible for humanity's passion for self limitation. When I reached my seventh year of teaching critical thinking on a college campus, I realized that dumbing down is something that comes all too easy. Perhaps a "slave chip" archetype plays over and over at the deepest levels of our consciousness. Perhaps dumbing down comes easier as we remember what happened way back in history (punishment from the gods), when we got "too close."

Yet our human growth may actually come from facing our past squarely. Accepting that we were created as slaves will not be fun. However, it might be the first logical step in breaking free of a highly limiting condition which has throttled our souls for at least 4000 years.

As George Santayana said: "Those who cannot learn from the past are doomed to repeat it."

When we look at the horrors of the Holocaust and the more recent horrors of Serbian "ethnic cleansing," we just might begin to understand that these actions emanate from a much darker history. *The Atra Hasis, the Karsag Epics, The Popul Vuh,* and even the *Old Testament* all speak of genocide and mass murder. *The Bhagavad Gita* has Krishna urging Arjuna to go into battle; however, Arjuna doesn't want to fight and has to be goaded by Krishna. Other sacred books tell of mass murder and genocide as if it were something holy.

Perhaps the time is right to consider that this was never a good idea – that entities which we thought were gods tricked us into doing their labor . . . and eventually tricked us into fighting their battles (see Sitchin's book *The Wars of Gods and Men*). With the scholarship of Zecharia Sitchin and other authors who are walking on the trail he has blazed, we might for the first time come to realize that what has been conditioned into us as being the truth actually cannot stand up to the light of truth.

The Russian mystic Gurdjieff claimed, "One cannot get out of prison until he is willing to admit that he is indeed in prison."

If Zecharia Sitchin is right, we were created – and highly conditioned – to be slaves. That's the bad news. The good news is that our slave masters departed long ago and we are, for the most part, free to search for the truth without fear.

Throughout history, many who have been conditioned to be slaves have been falsely forced to equate this slavery to holiness and spirituality. During the Inquisition, the Ruling Class of ersatz Anunnaki priests kept the passion for slavery-in-the-name-of-holiness alive. Today, Islamic and Christian fundamentalists alike rattle their swords in the name of "obedience equals freedom." But please remember, in reference to the above Gurdjieff quote, that blind obedience is the worst form of slavery.

Many have predicted that we are fast approaching a time where a passion for freedom will erupt throughout the world. At that time, we will boldly explore our true origins, accept what is valid, and reject what is not. I believe the person who is willing to accept that Zecharia Sitchin just might be on to something is centered in the truth. This coming period could be quite exciting. Hopefully, we will be able to break free of our slave programming. Should the Anunnaki return to discover that its creations are once again out of control, we need to stand up for ourselves and cast out the cosmic manipulators, the ones who tampered with humanity and its genetic code.

The paradox of it all is that because of this tampering we now have enough godly attributes as a species to be something beyond mere slaves. Like the people in the Tower of Babel incident, and thanks largely in part to Sitchin, we have begun to pull away the veil that hides the truth.

Once the truth about us is fully revealed, will our society squander it, cover it up, and refuse to accept it? Maybe. If that is the case, we will never advance as a species and are destined to repeat the same failure we experienced with the Tower of Babel.

On the other hand, if we become open to the truth and have scientists and media speak out (in addition to Sitchin) on these real and shocking discoveries, then we stand a chance to prove that we have matured enough to be more than just slaves for a slightly more advanced technological race.

To date, Mr. Sitchin has sold millions of books and his work still continues. In conversations I have had with him and in workshops of his I have attended, he has made it very clear that he does not pass on any of his research until he feels that he is rock solid in his documentation and research.

Zecharia Sitchin most certainly knows more, yet feels he must research further. Zecharia, when you finally feel completely sure and tell us, will we be brave enough to embrace what you have to say? If not, can we afford the price of not knowing?

The works of Zecharia Sitchin have allowed us to put many difficult puzzle pieces together regarding our fragmented and mysterious past. As long as he continues his work, and as long as people study his research in the future, we can expect a clearer picture to emerge of who we really are, where we came from, and where we might be going.

The Works of Zecharia Sitchin
1. *The 12th Planet*, 1976.
2. *Stairway to Heaven*, 1980.
3. *The Wars of Gods and Men*, 1985.
4. *The Lost Realms*, 1990.
5. *Genesis Revisited*, 1990.
6. *When Time Began*, 1993.
7. *Divine Encounters*, 1995.
8. *The Cosmic Code*, 1999.
9. Of Heaven and Earth, 1996. (Edited by Zecharia Sitchin)

Available from your favorite bookseller or from The Book Tree, PO Box 724, Escondido, CA 92033. 1 (800) 700-TREE, (24 hours).

CHAPTER TWO

THE FIRST DRAGON

Paul Tice

Dragon slaying goes to the very root of humanity. There is virtually no culture in the world without the dragon in its myth or folklore. The dragon could well be the most widespread symbol known to man. But what does it *mean,* and where did this symbol originate?

The most familiar place for us to look in the Western world is in the Bible. Here, combat with the dragon most always signifies the primordial struggle between the forces of order and of chaos. Later, in the prophetic sense, it refers to the end of the world battle where Satan, the dragon, falls. But this is not where the symbol began. Other older cultures must be considered.

The theme is found in India when Indra slays Vritra. The Roman St. Sylvester kills a dragon. The Hebrew Daniel destroys Bel, the Greek Hercules kills Hydra, the Babylonian Marduk triumphs over Tiamat, the Egyptian sun gods battle Apophis, Ahura Mazda slays Azhi Dahaka in Iran. In Japan the storm god, Susa-no-wo, rescues a princess by chopping a dragon to pieces. Dragon slaying is also referred to in *The Iliad,* by Homer.

The Middle ages and later give us dragon slayers in stories of the heroic St. George, Tristram, Siegfried, and King Arthur. And today, in modern Europe, an annual pageant recreates the slaying of dragons.

The theme is so powerful that it has followed us throughout history. Why? After all, no physical evidence for dragons has ever been found – no bones, fossils, *nothing.* Yet people throughout the world all seem to "remember" them. What is going on here?

A possible answer exists if we accept that we may have inherited some sort of "godly blood," or cosmic memory, from the gods themselves – gods who original-ly dealt with dragons in early myths. I could divert into support for this theory, but it is argued more convincingly by such esteemed researchers as Zecharia Sitchin, Neil Freer, Lee and Vivian Gladden, Christian O'Brien, John Cohane, Max Flindt and Otto Binder, only to name a few.

Evidence for alien or godly "blood" can also be found in the Bible. If *Genesis* is read carefully, one will notice two distinct and separate "creations." The second of these "creations" is the one falling under modern-day scrutiny. It is being close-ly examined in relation to the origins of us – modern *Homo Sapiens* – and points out a possible genetic connection to the gods. This connection is documented in religious stories, literature, and myths worldwide.

The point is, if we *are* related to the gods in such a way, we humans may have a tendency to "recall" similar myths (collectively speaking), including ones of dragons – even if we've never seen a real dragon. This includes primitive, isolated

Dragon Slaying: The oldest and most common myth in the world.

cultures that had many common myths between them, but no means of travel to spread such tales throughout the world.

To understand the dragon's origin clearly, we must start from the most basic concepts found in each myth:

The myths of dragon slaying follow a particular pattern. Dragons are usually found near water. That is its element – it represents both water and darkness. The dragon is causing trouble somewhere so a hero steps forward in an effort to slay it.

The hero is sometimes a god of light or a sun god. If he happens to be human, he's a representative of truth or light. It seems unlikely the hero will win, but he does – with the help of a secret weapon or special powers. He's then worshipped or becomes famous for the deed.

But where can we find the original pattern for this myth? What started the story? Where was the *first* dragon and who was the hero who slew it? These answers may be traced to the gods, *real* gods who were here on earth and fought with "dragons," as opposed to being mere "stories."

Many references about such gods point to the Babylonian creation myth called *Enuma Elish*. It means "When Above," and tells the story of the gods before their arrival on Earth. After their arrival we have the Old Testament, which states that "there were giants in the earth in those days . . ." Yet, the original Hebrew word *Nefilim* translates *not* to the word "giants," but to "those who came down."

When we examine the *Enuma Elish* and *Genesis* together, we find no inconsistencies and can actually see them overlap in a shockingly similar story. Another source for *Genesis* was the *Atra-Hasis*, already covered by Barranger in the previous chapter.

The *Enuma Elish* epic was translated from 7 clay tablets uncovered by various archaeologists between the years 1848-1929 (part of the 5th tablet is still missing today). These discoveries were made in what was once called Mesopotamia – the cradle of civilization. The tablets have received a great deal of attention from scholars worldwide for many reasons. To start, they strongly resemble the first 2 chapters of Genesis from the Old Testament, but were written long before it. Reading both provides a more complete and interesting story of our forgotten past.

Secondly, the story offers clues about the creation of the universe and our solar system, including the earth itself. It is within this creation story, but closer to the end, that we find our first "dragon."

To understand the first dragon, we must briefly tell this creation story, the *Enuma Elish*. It begins with "the divine parents" and their offspring. All that exists is Apsu – the male creative god, Tiamat, mother Earth (or the goddess of creation), and Mummu, their son.

A Babylonian depiction of Tiamat.

These male and female genders are probably just "terms" more than actual genders. The only known Babylonian depiction of the monster Tiamat is included here. It shows "her" with an unmistakable male appendage. This is interesting. We find the same thing in ancient Egypt, where the Earth is not female as we accept it today, but the sky is female, instead. She is Nuit and her male counterpart, Geb, is the Earth. Gender is important only insofar as it provides a context for the interaction of opposing or differing forces.

The *Enuma Elish* reveals Tiamat as the primeval saltwater ocean – possibly a massive, early version of planet Earth before some kind of catastrophe. She is a watery chaos, not being "formed" in the way we know now.

From here, scholarly interpretations vary but each leads to the appearance of our dragon. By comparing any existing interpretation with any other we can see how elusive myth can be (as there will be differences). Yet, between these views we may still sense an element of truth that has somehow been retained – as is often said about myths. Two of the more interesting views of the epic are those of Alexander Heidel and Zecharia Sitchin. They have their differences, as noted above, so to avoid confusion I will focus primarily on one.

Alexander Heidel's interpretation is found in his book called *The Babylonian Genesis* and is worth looking into, however, I will focus on Zecharia Sitchin's.

Sitchin, in his books *The 12th Planet* and *Genesis Revisited*, interprets Apsu, the primary god, as the Sun. He attributes this to Sumerian texts, where the word translates into "One Who Exists From the Beginning." Sitchin also tells us Mummu was the planet Mercury – "One Who Was Born," and that Tiamat was an earlier Earth. With Sitchin, the Sun, Earth, and Mercury are followed by the births of the remaining planets, although the exact process isn't revealed.

The epic continues, revealing that various generations of gods and goddesses are born. This could refer to the creation of additional planets or to beings who appear and start moving the planets around (much scientific and observable evidence exists for early cataclysmic events in the solar system). The universe becomes active with much noise from the young gods. It disturbs Apsu and Tiamat (the sun and Earth) greatly, for their peaceful existence is lost.

Apsu and Mummu come to Tiamat with a plan to quiet things once and for all. They will slay the young gods. Tiamat objects to destroying their own creations, but Apsu insists on doing it.

When the young gods hear the news they panic and run about aimlessly. They finally calm down and realize something must be done to save themselves. One of the young gods, Ea, casts a spell of sleep over Apsu to the point of his "death," and robs him of some important power he holds. This takes the most powerful entity out of the picture and puts a halt to the plan of destroying the young gods. The usurper Ea and his wife then give birth to Marduk – who will appear later as the first dragon slayer.

Tiamat is greatly distressed at the loss of her creator-god husband. Apsu was also the father and respected leader to many loyal gods. After his "death," some of the gods get wicked ideas. Led by Kingu, they go to Tiamat and convince her to avenge her husband's death. She could be next, being an equally powerful partner. And if someone killed or disabled *your* husband, who's job was to provide justice, wouldn't you then seek out that justice with the help of friends? They plan for battle. During the plan, Tiamat creates 11 different kinds of monsters to help them. One or more is a dragon:

With poison instead of blood she filled their bodies.

Ferocious dragons she clothed with terror,

She crowned them with fear inspiring glory and made them like gods.

Marduk and the dragon.

But they are up against Marduk – the new warrior god. These dragons fight bravely with Tiamat against Marduk but are defeated with her. Marduk kills her with a powerful wind and piercing arrow. He then splits her huge corpse in two, creating "heaven" and "earth" from the separate parts. All the rebel gods are taken captive and enslaved. The story continues into other areas, leaving the dragon behind.

Most references state that Tiamat herself was the dragon (and a male). This is not so. At no point in the original epic is it stated. In a tablet uncovered at Ashur, providing a similar version of the story, *the dragon is also clearly masculine* while Tiamat is feminine. She was a goddess of creation who made these 11 monsters, including the dragon. The dragon was *created* by her. As a result, later storytellers of the *Enuma Elish* may have found the dragon image helpful for listeners to visualize the events surrounding Tiamat. For example, the epic tells how Tiamat opened her mouth in an effort to devour Marduk – but failed.

Sitchin states that Tiamat, or at least half her body, is now the "earth" we stand on. The "heaven" part of Tiamat could well be the fragments in the asteroid belt, as he also explains.

Where is the dragon today? Myths throughout history most always place it in water. We find mythical "sea monsters" dating back to the early sea-farers, going up to present-day sightings of the Loch Ness Monster and a host of other likenesses. The dragon seems to have survived the battle, hiding deep within the confines of its mother. And with all of our mythologies there seems to be some kind of "hero" lingering within us, that still wants to slay it.

So where do we find a dragon in order to accomplish this? In Loch Ness? No. There is still no physical evidence. We are still searching for it, and it reflects in our beliefs. Down through our entire history, all heroic action seems to mimic this dragon myth. Many human actions mimic other myths as well. The best and most respected scholars in the field of mythology have stressed this fact, including Joseph Campbell. There seems to be an "archetypal blueprint" functioning in the background of our lives, and we unknowingly (for the most part) follow it. How did this come to be? Genetics might play a role. Some unknown genetic factor or an advanced but unconscious ability to tap into a mythologically-based "collective unconscious" (shared with the gods), could be involved.

The second creation of mankind (when godly genetic material was introduced to us) gave us a godly inheritance that allows us to "remember" dragons. Yet it was

Tiamat as "the dragon," attempting to devour Marduk.

done for the purpose of creating a worker, a "lullu," to help the gods. We not only helped them, but worshipped them. Neil Freer mentions in *Breaking The Godspell* that the original meaning of the word "worship" meant "to work for." We did both.

Early man had to be made smart enough to work for the gods, including mining their precious minerals, but stupid enough not to rebel (as the godly workers themselves had done).

Upon reflection, what do we see today? Any changes?? Many grudgingly trudge off to their jobs they dislike every day, wondering if there is some better way to live. We were not only "created" to work, but programmed for it.

During this process of creating a modern worker, did the gods of old genetically pass on to us some kind of hidden "memories"? It seems the answer is "yes," and the archetypes are at work within us. Including dragons. This is why we can't find a real "dragon" or dig up any bones.

The scholarly pundits of the day brush this off and tell us the dragon is simply a product of mythology and the human mind . . . The human mind? They mean the conscious part – that we made it up. But we don't know what 88% of the human mind is doing! We use only about 12% of it, and I must reiterate that archetypes are not conscious.

Dragons are our most powerful motif, something all cultures share through story and myth. This powerful, pervasive archetype makes it impossible for us to know exactly what the first dragon really was. There are no absolutes in myth. Myths are about gods and take place, for the most part, with little human involvement.

Gods are known to be from another realm, a realm which undoubtedly lacks physical proof as we know it. Champ, Ogopogo, and The Loch Ness Monster would all attest to this. Without physical proof, dragons are accepted as "imagined." Yet we've *seen* these things! Somewhere in the back of our minds lies the true answer.

Let's examine this. How do we actually view or perceive the dragon? What does it represent to us? The mind conjures up a depiction of evil – dragons are always mean, and are the enemy. Tiamat was a goddess of watery depths that were deep and dark (from here sprang the dragon); Marduk was a god of light, from above instead of below.

We associate darkness with evil, but darkness is just darkness. It is *we* who have made it evil. Like the Chinese yin and yang, there is a balance within us that is essential for our existence. One part is below the surface – our subconscious – and is shrouded in darkness. It is the home of our deepest mysteries, including the dragon. We fear it, so have labeled it "evil." Abraham Maslow once said, "above all, we fear the godlike in ourselves."

The dragon, hidden below the Earth's surface in its watery element. Occasional "sightings" have occurred throughout history.

The other half is the conscious mind that we understand more clearly, and are therefore more comfortable with. Many of us mistakenly believe that the conscious mind is all there is, and is cleverly responsible for our dragon stories. Not so. Myths and dragons are residents of the unconscious, and seem to fascinate us all.

Even if the dragon surfaces in our conscious minds only on occasion, it still has a reality of its own. It is a deeper, hidden reality. A memory. An archetype. And an inheritance.

Memories of the dragon have been passed on to us in a way we don't fully comprehend, only to be accessed today through imaginative tales. The human imagination keeps the dragon alive.

Einstein once said "Imagination is more important than knowledge." It could be so. We do not *know* that dragons exist, but we imagine them. We should never forget that the mind is very powerful, and to the human imagination, all things are real.

REFERENCES AND RECOMMENDED READING

1) Freer, Neil, *Breaking The Godspell*, Falcon Press, Phoenix, AZ, 1987.

2) Heidel, Alexander, *The Babylonian Genesis*, University of Chicago Press, 1963.

3) Hogarth, Peter, *Dragons*, Viking Press, New York, N.Y., 1979.

4) Holiday, F.W., *Creatures From The Inner Sphere* (formerly titled *The Dragon And The Disc*), Popular Library, New York, N.Y., 1973.

5) Huxley, Francis, *The Dragon*, Thames & Hudson, New York, N.Y., 1989.

6) Neumann, Erich, *The Origins And History Of Consciousness*, Princeton University Press, 1973.

7) Sheperd, Paul, *Nature And Madness*, Sierra Club Books, San Francisco, CA, 1982.

8) Sitchin, Zecharia, *The 12th Planet*, Avon Books, New York, N.Y., 1978.

9) Sitchin, Zecharia, *Genesis Revisited*, Avon Books, New York, N.Y., 1990.

CHAPTER THREE

PAST SHOCK
THE ORIGIN OF RELIGION AND ITS IMPACT ON THE HUMAN SOUL

JACK BARRANGER

Long ago something happened – something painful that few people possess the courage to look at it. Thousands of years ago a group of beings raped our souls. That not being horrible enough, this group of "advanced" beings claimed that this soul rape was good for us – that it was being done for our own good. These beings who raped our souls not only violated our spiritual sovereignty but also totally twisted the way we would view God. In fact, they increased the egregiousness of their violation by daring to tell us that they were God.

Julian Jaynes, author of *The Origins of Consciousness and the Breakdown of the Bicameral Mind,* claimed that this period was a period of intense psychosis for the emerging human race. The entities which created this spiritual rape had no sense of honor and did not respect the sovereignty of the human race. Instead, they trained this emerging species how to make war, how to work hard for their masters, and how to worship those beings as God. It was a horrible time. It was a time which created what we are experiencing today: Past Shock.

Future shock is a term invented by author/researcher Alvin Toffler to describe people's inability to cope with changes which are moving too quickly into their experience. Few people have a problem with future shock; it is now part of the public lexicon and well ingrained in American consensus reality. Past shock is not even close to being ingrained in consensus reality and probably won't for ten to fifteen years. However, the fact that it is not a part of consensus reality does not mean that Past Shock is not impacting humanity. Past Shock is impacting humanity much more than future shock, and it has been doing this for 4000 to 5000 years. While some people have some understanding of future shock, only a slight minority of humanity has an understanding of Past Shock.

However, the New Millennium, 2000 and beyond, promises to be a time in which the realities of Past Shock will begin invading our comfortable consensus reality. Then, the possibility of true liberation of the soul will begin. This will be an exciting time, but for many it will also be a terrifying time. What happened to us in the past is not pretty. Not is it edifying. However, facing it and eventually embracing it will begin individual humans and collective humanity on the collective path to transformation and liberation.

What exactly is it that happened to collective humanity thousands of years ago? What was it that was so horrible that collective humanity finds blocking its reality easier than embracing it? What was so shocking that the human mind and the collectivegarden of unconscious had to shield us so that our everyday lives could avoid the stress of remembering?

It lies in what we refer to as myth. Somehow calling our past history "myth" allows us to delude ourselves into thinking that what happened to us in the past was really something that was made up in people's heads. How comforting. How eventually destructive. It lies also within what we refer to as holy books. Within the *Old Testament, The Mahabarata, The Vedas, The Bagahvad Gita,* and many other holy books lie clues to what really happened in our past. Within *The Iliad, The Odyssey, The Epic of Gilgamesh, The Karsag Epics, The Atra Hasis,* and other epic poems from our historic past lie even more clues. However, in the past we, as a collective human species, have been most reluctant to follow where these clues have been pointing. That reluctance is finally beginning to wane.

With the waning of this reluctance, human beings singly and collectively have been looking at the clues and boldly inducing what these clues are pointing to.

Some approach this growing reality with great fear; others find themselves like Darwin as he began making discoveries about the origin of the species: he claimed, "With each new discovery I feel like I am committing murder." So it is with this writer. He grew up a comfortable and "certain" Christian; now he faces the horror of 5000 year old events and says, "If these events are true, the foundations of our society will be rocked."

What is it that happened thousands of years ago which – when discovered – will rock the foundations of our society?

The Foundation of Past Shock

Close to 12,000 years ago a race of technically advanced beings were on this planet. According to researcher/author Zecharia Sitchin, these beings came here 400,000 years ago. Both mythology and holy books support this: more than 30,000 written documents tell of a group of advanced beings who either came to Earth or already were living on Earth. These documents – especially the Sumerian, Assyrian, and Babylonian writings – claim that these beings came to mine precious metals. (Whether they came from outside Earth or from another part of this planet is not really an important issue at this point.) As the precious metals became more depleted, the work became more demanding, and the miners became mutinous. The *Atra Hasis* is amazingly clear in this area:

> Let us confront our chief officer
>
> That he may relieve our heavy work . . .
>
> Excessive toil has killed us,
>
> Our work is heavy, the distress much.

Atra Hasis

In this amazingly complex work, the *Atra Hasis* – and many other "mythological" works – tells of long negotiations to prevent a bloody mutiny. Finally, the advanced beings decide on a solution to their problems:

> Let a Lulu (primitive worker) be created . . .
>
> While the Birth Goddess is present,
>
> Let her create a primitive worker.
>
> Let him bear the yoke . . .
>
> Let him carry the toil of the gods!

Atra Hasis

Who was that primitive worker species? None other that what today is referred to as *Homo Sapiens Sapiens*. Yes, we are that species which was created to "do the toil of the gods."

What happened is the Anunnaki (as the gods were called in the Babylonian, Assyrian, and Sumerian epics) crossed its genes with the genes of an animal which most resembled them. That animal creature is what we now refer to as Homo Neanderthalis (Neanderthal Man). What the Anunnaki created from Neanderthal was *Cro Magnon* Man. For millions of years Neanderthal man had no written language or a capacity for language. *Cro Magnon* man had this capacity almost immediately. *Cro Magnon* Man was a genetic cross between the old level of man and the gods. If only we had been "good little workers" and stifled our god-like nature, we would not have brought down the wrath of the gods. However, something happened in this experiment which the gods were not counting on.

The Disastrous First Experiment

Like the disastrous "killer bee" experiment in South America more than twenty years ago, the genetic creation of humanity was not initially successful. (With the experiment that created the killer bee, the original intention was to cross the genes of a stronger bee with the genes of a bee which was more prone to work harder. Instead, they created a very rebellious bee with killer instincts and a strong tendency to migrate.) What the Anunnaki wanted was a docile primitive worker who was smart enough to do menial work but not smart enough to figure out that it was being exploited. Like the killer bee, *Homo Sapiens* turned out to be very bright, innovative, and quite hostile to the idea of doing menial work. This initial group was bright – probably much brighter than we are now.

As a species we were so bright that we severely frightened our creators. They wanted us to do menial work in the mines, and we wanted to discover the secrets of the universe. If our creators had possessed a shred of spiritual evolvement, they would have nurtured us from our inception. However, their only intent was to exploit us. Thus, conflict erupted.

We rebelled against the idea of doing *their* dirty work. Eventually, they wanted us to fight wars for them, and we rebelled against that (This is clearly recorded in the *Old Testament,* other holy books, and other ancient writings). This consistent theme runs through all of the past writings from various parts of the world. We were smart. Many of us might even have been smarter than our creators – and that must have severely frightened them. We started doing things which only increased their fears.

Zecharia Sitchin in *The Twelfth Planet* tells of a group of early humans in Babylonia which was so intelligent that it built a rocket ship capable of escaping the Earth's orbit. (Remember that the *Atra Hasis* and other ancient epics say that these gods claimed to come from the stars.) The gods were terrified that their newly created species might get back to their (the gods') homeland and tell of this infraction of the prime directive (not interfering with any indigenous species). Thus, the gods got together and worked out a plan to prevent this:

> Come, let us go down and confound their language, that they might
> not understand one another's' speech.

Genesis 11:7

According to Sitchin, the above is a much more accurate accounting of the Tower of Babel story. Early humans were not building a tower as much as they were building a launching pad. Our getting free was something they couldn't allow, and they came down upon us brutally. Thus began the foundation of past shock.

Another View of The Garden of Eden Myth – What Really Happened

Freud, Jung, and other founding fathers of psychology claim that even if the events of the Garden of Eden myth *didn't* happen, its impact as myth is still a gaping wound in our collective consciousness. Author Richard Heinberg in *Memories and Recollections of Paradise* relates how human experience is shaped by our guilt for having been thrown out of the Garden of Eden. The consensus reality is that God threw them out because they dared to eat of the Tree of Knowledge. This consensus reality goes on to state that this was the beginning of sin and that this is the point where the fall of man began. The problem with this consensus reality is that it is wrong. What this was, in reality, was the beginning of a spiritual rape from which we are still shuddering (or at least blocking out).

Something did happen in the Garden of Eden – something very horrible. One of the gods – a pernicious pretender to divinity who called himself Yahweh (Jehovah) – got totally caught up in his perverse paternalism and decided that Adam and Eve would be better off as cosmic pets. Their needs would be provided for as long as they remained at the level of domesticated pets.

Into the picture came a creature who figured Adam and Eve were getting a bad deal; these were intelligent creatures who were being told to keep their lights under a bushel. Throughout history this creature has been greatly maligned. Some even claim that it was Lucifer, but not even the *Old Testament* calls this creature by that name. Instead, the creature is referred to as the Serpent. In most mythology and holy writings the Serpent was known as the purveyor of wisdom. The Chinese saw both serpents and dragons as godlike, beneficial creatures who advanced humanity.

Adam and Eve expelled from the garden.

However, the Serpent has received very bad press from the Judeo-Christian segment of humanity. They saw – and continue to see the serpent as evil, even the devil. What the holy books do agree upon is that the Serpent was very beautiful. Actually, it is amazing how much of the original story is left in the *Old Testament*.

Adam and Eve are told by Jehovah that they can have everything they want as long as they don't eat any fruit from the Tree of Knowledge. (This is the equivalent of being told that you can have everything you want as long as you don't expect more than minimum wage and don't complain about the working conditions.) They were told that if they ate of the fruit of the Tree of Knowledge they would die.

This was a lie.

The Serpent appears and tells them that if they eat of the fruit of the Tree of Knowledge their knowledge will increase significantly. At this point, the Serpent is like Prometheus who is about to steal fire from the gods and give it to humanity. Unlike Jehovah, the Serpent is telling the truth. It's aim is not to destroy Adam and Eve as much as it is to liberate them.

What followed contributed greatly to past shock. Jehovah comes into the garden and says, "Where are you, Adam?" (something awfully strange to be stated by an omniscient God). Once Adam comes out of hiding, he observes a most traumatic event. Before Adam and Eve's eyes the Serpent is violently assaulted and mutilated (not something one would expect of an all-loving God, but unfortunately quite typical for the psychotic Jehovah). Other holy books describe an even more horrific fate for the Serpent: books like the *Jewish Pseudepigrapha* and *The Secret Book of John the Gnostic* tell of the Serpent brutally having each of its limbs hacked off.

Then, of course came all the other "prizes": women suffering in childbirth, men having to work by the sweat of their brow, and other multiplications of sorrows and pains. This was not the act of a loving god; this was the heinous act of a mentally tortured warlord who dared to tell his new creations that he was God. This expulsion from paradise was traumatic; however, it was also the beginning of humanity's liberation. (Ken Wilber's excellent book *Up From Eden* very effectively discusses this thesis. Rollo May also touches upon this thesis in *The Courage to Create*.)

Back to the Drawing Boards – The Spiritual Rape Intensifies

One theme stands out in the thousands of mythological and holy writings: our creators didn't like us as they originally created us. We were too smart and – from their perspective – too arrogant. We refused to become domesticated and we complained incessantly. The *Atra Hasis* tells of one of the gods who has had enough:

> The god Enlil said to the other gods: "Oppressive have become the pronouncements of Mankind. Their conjugations deprive me of sleep.

Being old enough to have suffered through three years of Latin studies, this writer found perverse humor in this. However, Enlil (whom many claimed was Jehovah) sees no humor in the wailing pronouncements of his newly created worker race. Something has to be done. A new creation is needed: a dumbed down human worker. They had already created spiritual rape by advancing us too quickly; now they were going to "de-advance" us.

The gods were mentally imbalanced Rodney Dangerfields who felt they just didn't get enough respect. Not only did they want workers who didn't complain, they also wanted us to venerate and revere them. While this is also a dominant theme in ancient writings, the one which best describes this "dumbing down" is the Mayan *Popul Vuh*. This holy book not only tells how the gods created humans as a work force but also how they had to keep recreating humanity:

> We have already tried with our first creations, our first creations, our first creatures, but we could not make them praise and venerate us. So let us try to make obedient, respectful beings who will nourish and respect us.

Thus, halfway around the world another group of gods were severely distressed with what they had created. Writing this off as "merely mythology" may create a "safe" certainty; however, it also keeps humans in a state of denial about what really happened to them in the past. Could it be that we turned out to be more intelligent than our creators? Is it possible that we were brutally treated because we refused to act like domesticated beasts of burden? According to the *Popul Vuh,* the dumbing down worked (in this case after five previous ineffective experiments). What exactly was it that they were trying to dumb down?

> . . . they saw and they instantly could see far, they succeeded in seeing, they succeeded in knowing where all is in the world. When they looked, they saw instantly all around them, and they contemplated in turn the arch of the heaven and the round face of the earth.

This is what had to be dumbed down. This is what frightened our creators. This was one of the most heinous acts of our misguided creators. We were genetically engineered and conditioned from birth to be creatures which would venerate and worship those who created – and spiritually raped – us. The *Popul Vuh* states how the gods were finally "victorious" in finally getting us to be obedient workers who worshipped our genetic creators as if they were the creators of the universe and the creators of the soul.

They were liars who were bored and used us as play fodder. They demanded worship because their souls were undeveloped. They made us fight their wars because they lacked the resolve and courage to fight them on their own. They made us build large edifices to praise them when they weren't even close to being worthy of our praise. We believed all of this because we had been so dumbed down that we no longer had the capacity to question those who committed this spiritual rape. We worshipped them because they treated us quite brutally if we didn't. We fought their wars because we knew that we would be slaughtered if we didn't. We praised them because that was what they wanted, and they got quite nasty if they didn't get what they wanted.

With every veneration and praise, we etched the cellular conditioning that these pretenders were God. We must have known that this was a sham because we resisted valiantly. Jehovah kept the Israelites in the wilderness for forty years so that he could have a third generation of killer warriors. No complaining Moses, no questioning Aaron – now they had Joshua who moved – and destroyed – without question. The violation of another people's sovereignty wasn't even questioned. Pretender god Jehovah ordained it, and the highly conditioned Israelites marched forward in their slaughter.

In the *Bhagavad Gita* and the *Mahabarata,* the warrior Arjuna wants to work out a peace with his enemies. However, Krishna at first persuades and then eventually goads Arjuna into fighting. How amazing that very few people are willing to see Krishna as the warmonger and Arjuna as the willing peacemaker. Because Krishna is seen as a god, most who read this account figure that he must have been right.

He wasn't. He was a technologically advanced being who was more interested in overcoming boredom and conquering territory. He wasn't in the slightest interested in the development of Arjuna's soul.

One only need look as far as the *Old Testament* to see an example of a god meddling in the process of peacemaking. Moses and Pharaoh had worked out a separate peace, but Jehovah would have none of it. He wanted slaughter – and most likely good theater. He wanted it so badly that he actually told Moses that he (Jehovah) had hardened Pharaoh's heart so that he might do battle. This, of course, led to the Red Sea slaughter which, according to one of David's Psalms, killed many on both sides. Yet Moses and Pharaoh had worked it out so this would have to happen. Jehovah probably needed to get his Israelites out into the desert so that he could whip them into shape and make damn sure that no peacemakers ever messed with his plans again.

This is rape – spiritual and physical. The conditioning has etched itself so deeply into our cellular memory that slaughtering by the Serbs in Bosnia and slaughter by both sides in Rhuwanda seems more like a natural reflex that a horrific act. The slaughter of 6,000,000 Jews was an easy process. The Christians smelled the bodies burning, but they could not or would not resist. This comes as much from war conditioning as slave conditioning.

By these "wonderful" gods we were beaten into submission if we dared to move out of our "slave chip" paradigm. 5,000 years later when the escape from the Sobibor concentration camp began (with most of the SS officers already killed), many simply could not run to their freedom. Many simply stood with heads bowed and prayed instead of running for freedom. Now that's powerful conditioning – conditioning which began 12,000 years ago and continues today like a slave chip playing in our brain.

What could they do to us then that caused us to be like that now?

An Offer You Better not Refuse – Jehovah's Devastating Covenant

Anyone reading Jehovah's words out of the context of the *Old Testament* would conclude that these were either the words of a raving lunatic or the rambling of someone no longer grounded in reality.

> If you follow my laws and faithfully observe my commandments, I will grant you rains in their season so that the earth shall yield its produce and the trees of the field their fruit. Your threshing shall overtake the vintage, and the vintage shall overtake the sowing; you shall eat your fill of bread and dwell securely in your land.
>
> I will grant peace in the land, and you will lie down untroubled by anyone; I will give the land respite from vicious beasts, and no sword shall cross your land. You shall give chase to your enemies, and they shall fall before you by the sword . . .
>
> I will look with favor upon you, and make you fertile and multiply you; and I will maintain my covenant with you. You shall eat grain long stored . . .
>
> *Leviticus* 26:3-10

These are the words of Yahweh/Jehovah to the Israelites. Sounds like a fair deal . . . right? Think for a moment about his. Consider for a moment that you own a thriving business; you are doing quite well on your own business initiative. In comes a well-dressed character and says, "I have a deal for you. If you will pay me $3,000 a month, I will make sure that your business continues to be successful."

You mention that your business is doing quite well on its own and that you don't need help from anyone. Then the man leans closer to you and says, "You don't understand. If you don't pay us the $3,000 each month, we're going to stand outside your door and tell people that we've been cheated. We're going to tell people that you won't honor your commitments and that your merchandise will break down within weeks. We're going to tell people that you're planning to go out of business within weeks and that your customers will be stuck with your product."

Immediately, you recognize the protection racket. These people are simply protecting you from the wrath that they intend to wreak upon you. You are gaining nothing, but you still have to pay for things to remain the same.

What does this have to do with Jehovah? Read on:

> But if you do not obey me and do not observe these commandments, if you reject my laws and spurn my norms, so that you do not observe all of my commandments and you break my Covenant, I in turn will do this to you. I will wreak misery upon you – consumption and fever, which cause the eyes to pine and the body to languish; you shall sow your seed to no purpose, for your enemies shall eat it. I will set my face against you; you shall be routed by your enemies, and your foes shall dominate you. You shall flee though none pursues.
>
> *Leviticus 26:14-17*

This is not a loving God who cares for his children. This is instead a highly manipulative warlord claiming to be God – a pretender to the throne. This is a petty entity incapable of gentle persuasion who is spiritually raping the people he claims to love.

But hang on, it gets "better":

> And if for all that you do not obey me, I will go on disciplining you sevenfold for your sins, and I will break your proud glory. I will make the skies like iron and your earth like copper, so that your strength shall be spent to no purpose. Your land shall not yield its produce, nor shall the trees of it yield their fruit.
>
> *Leviticus 26:18-20*

Sevenfold for your sins? Isn't that a bit excessive? What happened to an eye for an eye? This is seven days of detention for an offense requiring one day. This is swatting a dog seven different times for defecating once on the rug. Plain and simply put, this is cruel and unusual punishment – the kind of punishment meted out by vengeful people set on effecting a vendetta. Yet few – even in the Mafia – would mete out a seven-fold vendetta. This is the pronouncement of a very sick mind. Yet the Israelites were told by Jehovah that he was God – the only God worthy of being worshipped. By his very actions this pretender god was worthy of nothing but our contempt.

However, in this "deal" which Jehovah is forcing on his people, it gets even worse:

> And if for all that, you do not obey me, I will go on disciplining you sevenfold for your sins. I will loose wild beasts against you, and they shall bereave you of your children, and wipe out your cattle . . .
>
> . . . and if you withdraw into your cities, I will send pestilence among you, and you shall be delivered into enemy hands . . . You shall eat the flesh of your sons and the flesh of your daughters . . . I will heap your carcasses on your lifeless fetishes.
>
> I will spurn you. I will lay your cities in ruin and make your sanctuaries desolate . . . And you will scatter among nations, and I will unsheathe the sword against you. Your land shall become a desolation and your cities a ruin.
>
> *Leviticus 26:21-33*

Christian O'Brien, author of *The Genius of the Few,* claims that this covenant was disturbing for four reasons. (1) it was not a freely negotiated agreement between both parties. (2) The punishments proposed weren't even close to being civilized. (3) People other than the offenders would be punished – the good would have to suffer along with the bad. (4) Sin was being returned with evil – the punishment went far beyond the elements of the "crime."

However, understanding the dark side of Jehovah is essential. This is the entity who ordered a man stoned to death for picking up sticks on the Sabbath. This is the entity who threw poisonous snakes into a crowd of people – and killed many of them – simply because they were complaining. This is the entity who beamed with joy when he was told by one of his followers that this follower had impaled someone because he was not following the commandments.

This is also the entity – who despite claiming to be omnipotent – warned only a few people of an impending natural disaster and watched from above as millions of his creations died a terrifying death by drowning. (Even those who were saved couldn't have been that impressed because they were all numbed by drunkenness within a few days.) This is the entity which a majority of Americans worship as the God of the Christians and Jews.

This is also the god who spiritually raped us – his new creations – and created a past shock which lies deep within each and every one of us. This is the entity who insured that we would continue to worship him long after he departed. Exactly how did he do that? He and his cohorts created a highly effective system of conditioning which was so effective that its devastating impact has remained thousands of years after the departure of these pretender gods. What these pretender gods gave us to keep us in line was religion.

The Origins of Religion – Conditioning the New Creations to Be Spiritual Slaves

For just a couple of minutes, assume that you are very high up in the ranks of these pretender gods. You created the human race as a slave race – a herd to do your dirty work. With extended leisure time, you decided that you needed some warriors to help you conquer lands from the other entities who were mining the planet. When this became boring, you decided that you needed some entertainment – shall we say theater.

However, the warriors are refusing to fight. The workers are refusing to work and expending their energies instead in rioting. And – God forbid – many realizing that their lives don't show much promise are committing suicide. Just how do you make sure that your new creations fight your wars, do your dirty work, and stop committing suicide? After much discussion among the ranks, you finally come to an answer: create a religion.

In this religion you promise rewards in the next life – for eternity – as long as your creations play your game in this life. This means sweating and toiling without rebellion. It also means worshipping those who created you. For those who are just a tad unimpressed, you invent another place called Hell which promises great misery for eternity. To insure that they continue fighting in your wars, you promise that dying in war is an automatic ticket to heaven. Of course, the creators who claim that they are God in all other things get to pick and choose who goes where.

Those who commit suicide automatically go to hell. This insures that those humans who get depressed with their lot will remain with that lot, stuck fast in the hope that they will get to rest for eternity. To insure that they will spend eternity in Paradise, these badly conditioned and spiritually raped humans will spend their free time worshipping their creators and bending to their every whim. Because they have successfully blocked any memory of their spirit in the spiritual realms – and blocked all memory of past lives, these newly created humans have no way to prove whether this is real or false. Since this religion game is for eternity, one quickly realizes that it is best to play the game of the pretender gods.

Being one of these pretender gods, you had to be rock sure that your creations played your game according to your rules. To be absolutely sure that this happened, you create the ultimate cosmic "good cop/bad cop" game. You create a personal embodiment of a force that is trying to keep you in a state of sin (wanting to worship other gods, not obeying the dictates of the gods, not wanting to work, lusting after other women, etc.) You claim that this other entity wants your soul, and if this entity succeeds, you will spend all of eternity in hell. Thus, when you are told by one of these humans that he feels he is being exploited or that he wants to make peace with his enemies, you can tell him that this is the evil one working in his life and that he should pray to be guided by the forces of righteousness (that being you).

What is interesting in all of this is that when any of your rebellious forces experience pangs of conscience for what you are doing to them, you can condition them into believing that those who want to liberate them are evil. This is what happened with the Serpent in the Garden of Eden. This is what happened with Prometheus when he stole fire from the gods and gave it to humanity. This is what happened with the Norse god Loki who tried to throw a monkey wrench into the slave conditioning of the gods and made things so unbearable for them that they finally left.

These pretender gods might have left, but their conditioning remains. Inside each and every one of us is a slave chip which continues the conditioning of these despicable pretender gods. This slave chip is the result of many genetic experiments and thousands of years of religious conditioning. We play out that conditioning today as if these pretender gods were still in our midst. The singer of the song might be gone, but the melody lingers on with devastating impact.

A story is told of a soldier during the Korean War who was told to guard a certain area until he was relieved. What he did not realize was that his squad was quietly wiped out by the enemy. Thus, for three days he continued to guard the area. Finally into the fourth day he collapsed from exhaustion. When he woke up, he felt tremendous guilt because he had fallen asleep. He had no way of knowing that no one could possibly relieve him. So he continued in his guilt, somehow sensing that it was his fault that all of his squadron was killed.

Humanity is collectively like that soldier. As early humans, we were conditioned to worship interlopers and pretenders as God. These pretenders deserted us and left us to our own resources to survive because they no longer had need of us. That awesome and devastating conditioning remains with us. Like sheep we continue the patterns of worship. We still offer our bodies to fight the holy wars – and have hopes of paradise for participating in the slaughter. Our world of work still is not structured to serve the worker; instead god-like "superiors" are paid much more than they are worth because they can easily find worker drones who will work for much less than they are worth. We are so well conditioned that most any movement toward spiritual liberation will create guilt and a feeling that one is falling from the fold. We have been programmed well. We feel spiritually nourished to the degree that we remain spiritual slaves.

With no guidance from the pretender gods – or God himself – we burned John Hus at the stake, threatened Galileo with brutal torture, captured hostages from the embassy of The Great Satan, slaughtered whole cities in the name of Christ, raped and slaughtered the Indians we were trying to convert, and held heresy trails and painful executions for those who dared not believe. We continue to praise a long gone force "which saved a wretch like me." We see ourselves as sin-bound creatures. Those who "refuse" to see themselves as sin-bound still suffer from the dumbing down of the pretender gods. We walk this planet with a brain that is capable of moving mountains, yet we still use very little of it.

We are victims of a long past spiritual rape which has made past shock a part of our experience. The more we are willing to face what actually happened in the past, the more that we will be able to overcome this past shock and begin living as the humans that we are capable of becoming. The time to begin this exploration is now.

This was an excerpt from Barranger's larger book, Past Shock, ISBN 1-885395-08-6, which is available from The Book Tree 1 (800) 700-8733 or can be ordered from your favorite bookseller.

CHAPTER FOUR

UFOs: FROM EARTH OR OUTER SPACE?
AN INVESTIGATION INTO UFOs AND THEIR OCCUPANTS CONCERNING THEIR POSSIBLE INTER-DIMENSIONAL, EARTHLY ORIGINS

PAUL TICE

With each passing day our culture is exposed to more and more information about UFOs. We see more news reports, documentaries, magazine show segments and special programs on television about them. TV movies and theatrical films are continually being churned out, along with many important and revealing books. Magazines devoted exclusively to the subject have multiplied, more seminars and UFO-based "expos" are being done for the public. The list goes on and on.

It has reached the point where we are no longer asking if UFOs are real, but are instead asking, "Where do they come from?" and "Why are they here?"

The public mind-set is no doubt being conditioned to accept the reality of UFOs, and this conditioning has been happening for a number of years now. Only recently has the program been accelerated, so to speak, and I believe it is because we are on the brink of being told they are here. The conditioning is meant to soften what would otherwise be too heavy a blow. After a few more years we may be ready to know, as a society, the truth.

It seems clear that we are being visited by some type(s) of intelligent life. This is no longer clear to just crackpots and crazies, but clear to those who have had enough brains and concern to research the subject, or have had the luck (good or bad) to witness craft or experience what is called an abduction. *Something* strange *is* going on.

Like many others, I have experienced some strangeness of my own. I grew up in western Massachusetts and experienced many sightings in a remote area of a small town, especially between the years 1967-69, during what is called a UFO "wave" or "flap." Although rather young, I was old enough to realize that nothing *man-made* from this earth could do what these objects were doing. My impression was that they simply had to be from outer space. I set out on a life-long quest to discover what I could about these "visitors."

After much research and many years later it seems that my extraterrestrial explanation may not be the only answer. But neither can it be *completely* ruled out. Remember, we must keep an open mind if we are ever to discover the truth.

The purpose of this work is to examine where UFOs may truly be coming from. My opinions are only my opinions, and I do not claim to have a monopoly on the truth. There are a number of intriguing possibilities as to the origin of UFOs, but the strongest and most valid one, to me, is that they originate from right here on earth, and have been with us from the beginning.

PART ONE
The Extraterrestrial Hypothesis

This hypothesis usually begins by stating that there are billions of galaxies out in space and literally billions of stars within *each one* of these galaxies. To think that we are the only place anywhere to have developed intelligent life is practically ludicrous. In fact, the odds of us being totally alone are almost not worth considering – the deck is stacked immensely in favor of there being not one but many other forms of intelligent life in the universe.

So we come to the many UFO sightings and encounters on our small planet. Looking out into the depths of space and considering the odds just mentioned, one is apt to believe that these craft and beings do come from somewhere "out there" –

in space. But where? Are there any known reports that might indicate exactly where these ships or beings come from?

Yes, there are documented reports. We will go over some of the better known reports in support of the extraterrestrial hypothesis.

The Betty and Barney Hill Star Map

Possibly the best known case in support of the E.T. hypothesis. This couple claimed to have been abducted in the White Mountains of New Hampshire in 1961. They were driving in an isolated area, had a UFO sighting, then realized they were "missing time" (much more time had elapsed, almost instantly, than they had perceived). This experience with time has become a common element in many abduction cases. They also found themselves 60 miles south of their previous location. Was this some kind of shared delusion, and was the UFO they sighted a shared hallucination? Most likely not. The object they witnessed was independently picked up by radar at Pease Air Force Base, giving support to their story.

Soon after, the couple began to experience various physical and psychological troubles so underwent hypnotic regression in an effort to help uncover the root of the problem. Each detailed a separate, identical story of being abducted by small gray beings. They were examined by these creatures and released, but before being released Betty was shown a "star map" inside the saucer. She was shown this map after asking one of the entities where they were from. She recreated the map under hypnosis, which was later researched by a school teacher named Marjorie Fish. Ms. Fish investigated all known stars within 55 light years of our own sun that were considered ideal for supporting life, and came up with a 3-D match to Betty Hill's map. This match places the entities in the Zeta Reticuli star system, 220 trillion miles away. This is equal to approximately 37 light years away, making it a close neighbor. Zeta Reticuli is also a double star system, containing two stars similar to our sun that could support earth-type life.

If you have not read *The Interrupted Journey* by John Fuller, which gives the full account of this story, you are missing one of the best and most convincing abduction stories available.

The Hill case goes far in bolstering the idea that abductions by aliens do exist, but it does not necessarily prove that these aliens are from Zeta Reticuli or anywhere in outer space. That is the more popular notion, but another alternative exists. This alternative is that such "aliens" could be ultraterrestrial rather than extraterrestrial – meaning they are from the earth rather than outer space.

Jacques Vallee and John Keel, among a handful of others, give highly convincing arguments for ultraterrestrial origins. Vallee uses Hill's star map as an example for his own theory, stating that there are innumerable (and possibly infinite) angles that could have been used by Ms. Fish concerning the *other* 46 possible life-supporting stars in the area, and that Zeta Reticuli could only be the first one that she had stumbled across. He also points out that the two Zeta Reticuli stars have a distance between them on the map that was drawn so far off from scale, that this star map would have been totally useless for navigation. And, he asks, why was the map drawn or shown from an angle that does not correspond to any known celestial object? In other words, there is no reference point. In addition, we humans do not even use maps when navigating space – it is all done by computers and telemetry. So why would an advanced race be using them?

Vallee answers this question by stating that these aliens *wanted* Betty Hill to see the map, to make her *think* that these creatures were from somewhere out in the universe (but really weren't).

Cover Stories and Diversions

Many, many encounters with "otherworldly" creatures have occurred over the years where people have been told by the aliens that they come from all kinds of places all over the galaxy and universe. Some have said Venus, others Orion, still others claim Clarion as their home, or Lanulos, or the Pleiades, or one of a multitude of places that are ridiculously false or imaginary.

I believe, like Vallee, that information like this is part of a continuous diversion. It is much like the WWII example given in his book *Dimensions*. The British were trading a German general for war prisoners and were driving him to make the swap. Before doing so, however, they changed road signs ahead of time along the way, causing the general to report to his High Command, once exchanged, that all of the war machinery and armies he had seen along the way were in a completely different area. This distracted the Germans away from Normandy where, in fact, he had really been near and where the successful invasion of Normandy took place.

These entities do not want their cover blown. They want the believers of this phenomenon to think they are from outer space. Why? Because if we discover that they are really residents of *this* world, but in a neighboring dimension, they could become vulnerable. They would rather that *we* remain vulnerable, as we have been for centuries. And as long as we are kept ignorant of their true origin we will remain vulnerable to them and their manipulation.

Pleiadians and Billy Meier

This is one of the most interesting and ongoing UFO sagas out there. The bottom line question is this: Are there Pleiadian entities visiting the earth? When you think about it, it becomes the same question as: Is Billy Meier a fraud or is he for real?

Incredibly convincing arguments exist on both sides of the coin. Despite all of the positive "evidence," one should not accept the reality of the Meier case until the work of Kal Korff is studied. Unfortunately, Korff's work is largely overshadowed by the hoopla of Meier devotees who swear that the Pleiadians are here.

A number of people portray Meier in a positive light – Randolph Winters, Jim Dilletoso and Gary Kinder, to name a few. Their work is more readily available and more known than Korff's, stating that Meier began his contacts with the Pleiadians in Switzerland back in the 1940's – both physically and telepathically. Since then he has amassed many excellent, clear photographs of what seems to be flying objects and written out thousands of pages of transmitted wisdom and prophecies. Is it all a hoax?

Back in the 1970's a man named Bill Jenkins had an immensely popular radio show called *Open Mind* on ABC Radio. One of the show titles was "The Billy Meier Hoax." That was the title of the program. In spite of the ever-present "evidence" that supports it, many of the top UFO experts in the country were on the program and unanimously concluded Meier to be a hoax without any reservations. It seemed to be common knowledge at that time. But since then, a cult following has amassed itself around the case and virtually drowned out what was once considered common knowledge.

And today, people will hate me for even mentioning the name Kal Korff. I was reamed out by at least 5 Meier supporters at an International UFO Congress for selling Korff's video at my Book Tree booth. These people did not welcome an opposing view because they already knew "the truth." Korff actually went to Switzerland, under cover, and became a member of the Meier group. When there was a supposed landing that everyone became excited about, he was the only one who went to the site and took soil samples (which had to be done under the cover of darkness). Once tested, no anomalies in the soil were found.

Korff returned to precise locations of previous Meier photographs and retook photos to check the landscapes for consistency. In one case, a tree that should have been present was no longer there. Asking neighbors who lived closest to where this tree should have been, he was told that no such tree ever existed there. Later, Meier and his people explained that the tree was once there, but had now been teleported back into time by the Pleiadians.

Also, Meier claimed to have been taken on a journey to Venus by these friendly Pleiadians, where he took further photographs as "proof." Korff found an identical picture of Venus, matching one of Meier's, out of NASA files. Korff also explains a number of interesting photographic tricks and how they could have been used by Meier – for instance, many of the photographs of UFOs were taken into the sun, which could easily hide supporting objects. Korff also uses a mathematical formula to determine the size of objects in pictures, and many of Meier's craft do not measure up. Most people do not know this side of the Meier story, and when they *are* told, usually do not welcome it.

At a Mutual UFO Network (MUFON) meeting in Burbank, California in 1995 Mr. Korff was treated with extreme rudeness by a handful of people in the audience, who heckled and insulted him. The meeting had opened with Randolph Winters showing some of Meier's photos, and time was also given to Meier proponent Jim Dilletoso. But when the audience heard Korff they acted (for the most part) like a large group of kids who had just been told that Santa Claus does not exist. The place turned into a total zoo, and was the most chaotic MUFON meeting I'd ever attended. It is still talked about to this day. Many believers simply did not want to hear Korff's message, no matter how well-researched it was.

The point is, there may not be any Pleiadians. At all. I'm serious. No Pleiadians from outer space. Simply accept this as a *possibility;* that is all I'm asking here. Don't rush off the deep end with all the hype. Look, learn and investigate deeper. *Then* decide.

The Theories of Zecharia Sitchin

Sitchin is one of the few people in the world who can translate ancient Sumerian writing (cuneiform). This is the oldest known writing on the planet, and many of our myths and legends sprang directly from what the Sumerians wrote in the ancient Middle East.

Sitchin uses these texts to reveal the story of Niburu, the 12th planet. *The 12th Planet* is also the title of his first book, which is highly recommended. This planet is in a very elongated orbit of our sun and only reappears every 3,600 years, claims Sitchin. It is the home of the gods, the ones who came down and taught us how to write, start cities, cultivate crops, map the heavens, and do everything else which earmarks "modern civilization." These gods could well explain the overnight explosion of civilization that humans experienced at this time.

These beings displayed great powers and were clearly not human. Yet they still quarreled among themselves, were spiteful, jealous, selfish, petty, and warlike. Sitchin claims they tampered with humanity, genetically, and passed some of their godly traits on to us – both good and bad. We've created medical breakthroughs, tremendous cities, and wonderful modern inventions, yet wage war upon each other continuously and are harming nature terribly. It all came with progress.

When the gods arrived we were primitives, and at one with nature. We were *part* of nature and in harmony with it. But both our genes and consciousness have been altered, due to their tampering. We genetically inherited progress and technology, and no longer fit perfectly into nature's scheme. It was Plato, probably the wisest philosopher who ever lived, who said, "Man is poised half way between the animal and the gods." I believe we are exactly that – half animal and half god, a hybrid race. So does Sitchin. He believes this hybrid race was created for the purpose of slavery. The gods were here for the mining of precious minerals. Their workers grew tired of the hard labor and mutinied. An answer had to be found, some way to do the work, so they chose to create a new race from the local primitives by mixing the primitive genes with their own godly DNA. Done to the proper amount (after some trial and error) the new race was created smart enough to do the required work, but dumb enough not to revolt (as the gods had done). Look around yourself today, and really think. Examine your job and those of others and ask yourself if much has changed since this "slave race" was created.

These gods were called "Nefilim," meaning "those who came down." Instead of coming down from another planet, I believe it equally plausible that they came down from a higher dimension. We have yet to see this "12th planet" in light of all the sophisticated telescopes and advanced space-monitoring gear that we've developed. All we have today is subtle, indirect evidence that this planet could exist – based on orbital variations of the outer planets. Some "notables" claimed it was going to be the Hale-Bopp comet, which appeared in 1997, or that Hale-Bopp was a precursor, by 7 years, to Niburu (the 12th planet). Time will show (in 2004) that this is not the case. During all the pre-Hale-Bopp hype, I correctly predicted the comet as *not* being Niburu (in an earlier edition of this work). And I'm also telling you that it is not a precursor. I'm amazed that people will still follow, believe and accept those as credible who have spread such fantasy crap to the public.

This planet could indeed exist, but why haven't we seen it yet? Sitchin claims it's because it's too far out in its orbit at this particular time. I'm open to the idea. I spent 10 days with him in early 1996 exploring the Mayan ruins and pyramids, followed by additional trips with him to Turkey, then Israel, then back to the Yucatan again. Having known him and read his books, it's clear that he does not make any claims until he has fully researched things first. The work of Zecharia Sitchin is the most scholarly available concerning the ancient astronaut theory and should not be ignored.

Entire books could be written on Sitchin alone. He has been mentioned here because I believe the extraterrestrial theory should not be completely thrown out the window. I do not try to discount the E.T. theory totally – I'm the first to admit that we do not have definite answers. There could be extraterrestrial visitors that are also inter-dimensional. Or both such entities (extraterrestrial and inter-dimensional) could exist separately.

Regardless of Sitchin's work, it is still hard *not* to accept the ultraterrestrial view – either in addition to, or apart from it. The following section will discuss why.

PART TWO

The Ultraterrestrial Hypothesis – Reasons for Ultraterrestrial Visitors

The visible light spectrum and all of reality, for that matter, goes far beyond what we can see. And some of what we *can* see or experience remains a mystery to us as well. What is gravity? We have no idea. What is electricity? We don't know. We know how to use it, but don't ask anybody what it is. We still know very little about the world we live in, although few of us, including scientists, will 'fess up and admit it.

This larger reality, which exists all around us, has incredible implications. We are like fish in water. Seeing a UFO is like having a fish witness a person sticking their hand into a pool of water in the stream. Withdrawing the hand will make the fish believe the hand no longer exists, since it is no longer present in their "world." But the hand still exists – it's attached to an entity in some other reality. This entity chose to intrude on *your* reality (the fish's) just briefly. The person was possibly concerned about something in the fish's environment and sought to investigate or change it.

Now note, for instance, how a huge UFO wave followed the first nuclear tests in New Mexico and continued into the 1950's. After the bombs were dropped in Nagasaki and Hiroshima, the world was inundated with UFO sightings occurring on the same latitude coordinates around the world. We *attracted* them.

The UFO crash at Roswell in 1947, which the military officially announced, then retracted and claimed was a "weather balloon," was probably the result of UFOs investigating the New Mexico nuclear bomb tests (during a thunderstorm). This is where all of our testing took place. Also note how worldwide sightings continually occur at 1) nuclear power plants that provide the material, and 2) military bases that house the nuclear weapons. If one follows the situation, it is quickly realized that this is no coincidence.

We know so little of the totality of reality. We do not know what these aliens do – which is that nuclear detonations cause a dangerous ripple effect into other dimensions. It's okay for us to jeopardize our reality, just don't go messing with theirs. They would like to put a stop to that without revealing themselves to us. Otherwise, as mentioned previously, they would become vulnerable to a race of people that cannot be trusted. Face it, if you were them, would you trust us? Human nature can turn on you and do terrible things – just look at the world we live in! If we are kept fighting among ourselves, as we have done for centuries, we will never catch on to them.

I have often stated that finding the true nature of these entities is much like discovering that you've got rats in your basement. They stay expertly hidden, are crafty, and only come out at night. But as their numbers and activities grow, more clues emerge. Things like gnawed boxes, strange rustlings in the night, or stumbling across one that has wandered briefly into sight. We are now at the point of making this shocking "rats in the basement" discovery concerning these alien entities.

They're here. They always have been. It, or they, have been "just next door," and we will soon uncover the means to get there – just as *they* know how to get *here*.

This helps to explain how UFOs are often witnessed vanishing into thin air. They "melt" into that other dimension, right before people's eyes. Vallee believes they are part of an overall "control system" over us, molding us in ways that serve them. John Keel has often repeated the Charles Fort quote, "We are property." They basically "own" us.

With Us Since the Beginning

If this is so, what is the evidence? Let's look at history. Is the abduction phenomenon new? No, it is not. For centuries, stories have been told of people who were abducted by fairies, elves, or wee folk, where people were "missing time" once returned, and experienced a whole list of common occurrences with modern UFO abductions. Were these past cases really just myth or folklore, as academia would have us believe? Or did they actually happen?

When one studies mythology and folklore, interesting patterns are found that shape themselves over long periods of time. These patterns are found in all cultures. Legends and sacred texts from India speak of "flying machines," or "vimanas." Many books have been written on flying saucers in the Bible and from the middle ages we find dozens of wood-cuts showing strange objects in the sky. Stories concerning them were written down by confused and curious observers.

Many rational people discount the possibility of flying saucers in the Bible, yet with no advanced technology at the time, the language used to describe what would have been a UFO is exceedingly accurate. The deeper you look into it, the more plausible it becomes that UFOs and their occupants have been with us throughout history.

The Hidden Dimension

A good illustration of their continued presence would be that of the two-dimensional world viewed from the 3-D perspective. Two dimensions would encompass no more than the print on this page. These letters (if capable) would only be conscious of events occurring on the page, not above or around it. They would not be aware of your "reading" them, nor of any movements of other activities taking place in the room around them. If you were to take a safety pin and move it through the page, they would not see it coming. However, once it touched the page and entered their reality, they would be conscious of it. They could (if capable) see, hear and touch the pin as it poked a hole in their reality. This is how we experience UFOs and alien beings. When they choose to enter our reality, we see them. Otherwise, they are all around us and we don't experience them because they are above us in a higher dimension.

They can and do see everything that happens in this world. And they do *not* want to lose that advantage. To them, it is worth protecting.

Ancient cave painting discovered on the Tassili plateau of the Sahara. Called "The Great Martian God," it is the largest prehistoric painting known, being 18 feet high.

As we progress as a species we will stumble onto the doorway to higher dimensions. In fact, we may have already done so but the fact is being covered up. *This* is the one secret that is even bigger than the existence of UFOs. This fact, and humanity's access to it, would blow the lid off our reality and the minds of everyone in it. It would totally shake the foundations of our entire system down to its very core, and a new paradigm would have to begin.

World leaders know that this should not happen quickly. The powers that be enjoy owning all the oil companies, power companies, banks, and everything else that fuels our current system. New and better possibilities would destroy their control.

Our world leaders (the human ones) are not politicians. They are *money peo - ple*, some of whom are involved in secret societies. They, and only they, are in contact with entities from a higher dimension. These people pull the strings for our true "masters." It *is* a conspiracy. Two groups have conspired to share control of this world for their own separate agendas. Having money people run things for these aliens is a necessary safeguard. Both sides do *not* want this information known because it serves their aims and keeps each in control of their own "realm."

Each dimension effects the other, but the higher dimension is clearly in the driver's seat. Our human masters are only the puppets of higher dimensional entities. Politicians are puppets of the puppets. The world's money is used to keep the current system running – as inefficient and damaging to the environment as it is. As we continue to damage and pollute our world, it is beginning to effect the higher dimensions. This means certain limited changes must be engineered while preserving the number one objective – keeping the populace ignorant. If this succeeds, then the system (and its secret alliance) is preserved. The entire truth of who we are and what we can become is being covered up for the sake of power mongers.

Custodians, Rats and Cosmic Tricksters

William Bramley, in his acclaimed book *The Gods of Eden*, called our alien counterparts the "custodians." Based on how they oversee us from a higher dimension, I believe this term to be accurate. It brings to mind Vallee's "control system."

This control system, according to Vallee and Keel, operates directly on our three-dimensional reality *and our perceptions of it.* This control system includes the manipulation of the world's most powerful people, who do not want to lose their power should the truth be let out. That truth being that another reality exists next door.

Our access to this other reality or dimension would change everything on a physical scale, and mental scale as well. It would alter our consciousness. I would agree with world leaders in stating that changes in this direction really *should* happen gradually. This would allow humanity to avoid the worst case of culture shock imaginable. We must work in this direction because continuing on our current, materialistic path will not only mess up our world further, but will mess up the higher worlds as well. These aliens know this and are calling the shots. The trick is to keep the masses ignorant here and bring us up slowly into accepting their existence. If done their way, they'll still be in charge when it's over.

Watch television lately? Aliens are *everywhere*. This is no coincidence. Do some research. Find out who owns the major broadcast networks – who *really* owns them. Don't stop at the first company name. Find out who owns *them*, and keep going till you get to the top. Figure it out.

Photo taken by author in Feb., 1996, of the Pyramid of the Moon in Teotihaucan, Mexico. The object above the pyramid was not visible when photo was taken.

In the meantime, a hidden part of our world is teeming with UFOs and other forms of unseen life. The most recent development comes from a man named Jose Escamilla, and his discovery of the "rods." These cylindrical rods fly through the air at incredible speeds and can only be picked up by high-speed cameras. They range in size from one foot to a hundred feet in length, while leading scientists grope at straws, trying to discount them and the impressive, undeniable evidence amassed by Escamilla. In the 1950's a man named Trevor James Constable developed a form of infrared photography that repeatedly revealed UFOs flying in the California desert that would otherwise have remained invisible. And tourists in Yellowstone National Park have found unusual flying objects in pictures taken on ultra-violet film. These "things," these objects, are all around us and we don't even know it! If we had any idea at all what really surrounds us, it would probably scare most us half to death.

Many unidentified craft are witnessed as balls of light which transform themselves into solid looking mechanical objects, or as mechanical objects which fade out into nothingness. They seemingly go through all visible phases of our electromagnetic spectrum while moving between dimensions.

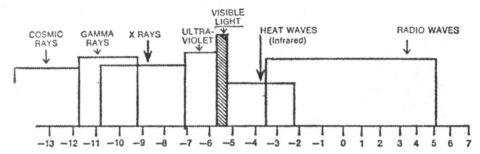

Chart of the electro-magnetic spectrum, or "superspectrum."

Essential reading on the manipulation of these energies is John Keel's 1975 book entitled *The Eighth Tower*. In it he describes how many parts of our energy spectrum operate. He refers to it, as a whole, as the "superspectrum." Control over this superspectrum is maintained by entities referred to by Keel as ultraterrestrials – being from this world as opposed to extraterrestrials, which are not.

We humans are in no position to fully understand the superspectrum, much less manipulate it. Because of this, everything that we see or experience can be manipulated, and possibly created, by outside forces. Want a vision of the Virgin Mary? No problem. What about a Bigfoot or one of those lake monsters? Anything to keep us guessing. The trickster does surface in these "otherworldly" entities – after all, most people haven't got the foggiest idea about what is really happening here, so these manipulators can't resist having a little fun, I'm sure.

Like the time Joe Simonton was visited by a UFO in his back yard. An alien creature disembarked and presented him with a highly important gift from another world – pancakes! That's right, Joe got pancakes when he was probably expecting an important practical device or a special, informative introduction to another race. These renowned pancakes were shipped to various labs around the world for analysis and it was discovered that they were perfectly normal pancakes. Sorry Joe. I recall seeing a picture of the notable UFO expert J. Allen Hynek, posing with one of the famous pancakes. It was extremely unimpressive – flat, crusty, and full of holes.

John Keel tells of showing up at a certain hotel completely at random during the height of his UFO and superspectrum investigations to find a number of messages waiting for him at the front desk. Somebody was showing off. There was no way anyone could have known he would be there – even *he* didn't know it, until he suddenly decided to stop.

Keel also tells of the mysterious "men in black" that show up to harass people who have experienced UFO sightings. These men in black are known to show up even before witnesses have a chance to report their sightings! The witnesses are usually warned to say nothing about what they have seen, or else. The MIBs often arrive in older model black automobiles (usually Cadillacs) that show no sign of age – in perfect mint condition. Some people have reported no seams whatsoever on the vehicles, which is a trait often reported by those claiming to have been inside a UFO.

Keel chased one of these vehicles onto a dead-end road only to discover, once he rounded the corner, that the vehicle and its occupants had totally vanished.

The men in black are commonly described as having olive skin, oriental features, and usually wear dark glasses in addition to their clothing. Whenever evidence is recovered by a witness in connection to a UFO sighting (and this *has* happened), one or more of these men will surface almost immediately to buy back or steal the item. Keel says this scenario is continually repeated and cites examples in his book *The Eighth Tower.* Many of the cases also reveal these MIB to be threatening and intimidating.

Are these men in black normal people? Have you noticed such people living near you, as neighbors? Not likely. Think very carefully as to who and what they might really be.

When Keel finished his most painstaking years of research, he concluded that no evidence exists for UFOs being extraterrestrial. What is interesting is that this is the same conclusion arrived at by Project Blue Book. Blue Book, however, said that UFOs were the result of people hallucinating or mistaking known objects for unknown craft. Keel agrees with Blue Book that UFOs are not extraterrestrial, but is at odds with their explanation. According to Keel, UFOs are the result of earthbound spirits that have been with us from the beginning of time. They are illusion-prone entities that know how to manipulate matter, energy and time. This goes far beyond Blue Book's limited view of "hallucinations" and human error.

A Larger View of Reality

For their own ends, these entities continue to frighten, confuse, and mislead the human race and have no intention of stopping. The means by which they manipulate these energies and keep us confused is with the so-called superspectrum. This total spectrum of energies consist of gamma-rays, ultra-violet rays, gravity, infrasonic sound, various magnetic fields, radio waves, microwaves and more. These energies, in some form or other, account for all paranormal activity.

Things like ghosts, ESP, prophecy, Bigfoot and UFOs have a stronger existence outside of our space-time continuum – making them extra*dimensional*, not extra*terrestrial*. They are not a normal part of our reality, so are not subject to our natural laws. Therefore, UFOs can change shape, color, or brightness easily as they traverse through the visible part of our electro-magnetic spectrum. They often vanish before people's eyes when they reach frequencies that we cannot perceive. This is not magic, or make-believe. It is science. We may not understand it yet, but it is still science.

This brand of science is so elusive to us because these manifestations involve the perceptions of the human mind more than the "nuts and bolts" proof that everyone is trying to uncover. Sure, these nuts and bolts exist and we can scientifically examine material objects. But when these objects appear only occasionally in our world, it is hard to pin them down long enough for scientific scrutiny.

And, from their end of things, it may be just as difficult for the alien creatures to share anything with us at all since we operate from within such a comparatively narrow spectrum. In his 1995 book *Breakthrough*, Whitley Strieber says, "Because of the way we are, trapped in linear time and enslaved to our narrow view of the physical, the visitors cannot really share with us the way they want to, that is in every possible way. A great deal of the strangeness of the relationship, I suspect, has to do with our ability to see only a small part of what is actually unfolding between us."

The implications of this quote are phenomenal. If true, these "visitors" can do many kinds of things all around us and never be noticed – unless they make a special effort to show themselves. It could be that all kinds of tricks and manipulations are being perpetrated upon us, we then live out the results blindly, and never know the actual cause. So, to bring back the "rats in the basement" syndrome, as mentioned earlier, we simply do not know they are here, doing their dirty work.

> "It is being discovered that we are manipulated by someone or something unknown, a power which accords us little respect and uses us for its own ends in the very same way we use animals . . . If this discovery proves to be legitimate, although this state of affairs has existed since the beginning of time, humanity is in for a collective shock when it realizes exactly what has been going on."
>
> *– Salvador Freixedo*

Due to scientific advancements, we (more educated) humans now think in terms of multiple realities. We must now wonder which reality "they" belong to, since ours is clearly not the only one.

Jacques Vallee's opinions also fall directly in line with this view. He believes that UFO sightings have strong links to religious apparitions like the Virgin Mary and supernatural creatures like fairies and elves. He believes they all pop in from a neighboring dimension or reality.

Centuries ago many cultures experienced a rash of "little people" sightings much like the way we encounter UFOs today. Vallee believes that what we experi-

Flaps from the past: Zeppelins and "little people."

ence from this other reality depends much on the current culture. Today we are more technological – thus, we see flying machines instead of strange little people.

At the turn of the 20th century many rural Americans witnessed flying airships, much like zeppelins, long before such things were invented. Were they just a more primitive version of UFOs for a slightly less advanced culture? Will we, in turn, be making and flying modern UFOs some time in the future? Many think that is precisely what is happening, and has been happening, at secret government test sites like Area 51.

When you research the older reports of these "little people," which is how many modern aliens are described, we find similar reports of abductions. Many of them. People who encountered the wee folk also experienced lapses of missing time – losing all track of it, then resurfacing in a familiar place hours or even days later. Sound familiar? These are identical to reports of modern UFO abductions.

In Vallee's own words we find his viewpoint explained clearly. He says,

> "I do not believe any more that UFOs are simply the spacecraft of some race of extraterrestrial visitors. This notion is too simplistic to explain their appearance, the frequency of their manifestations throughout recorded history, and the structure of the information exchange with them during contact . . . My own private conjecture, which deviates considerably from the accepted dogma among UFO believers, is that *we are dealing with a yet unrecognized level of con - sciousness, independent of man but closely linked to the earth.*"

That means something terrestrial. *Not* extraterrestrial.

Modern Pioneers

Vallee and Keel are pioneers – the first to have put forth the ultraterrestrial argument with candor and intelligence. Three other brilliant people have supported this view nicely (I may be missing others; I apologize if that is so).

The first is a man named Salvador Freixedo, from whom I have already quoted. It is said that he has influenced the work of both Vallee and Keel. Born in Spain, his books remain in the Spanish language except for one – *Visionaries, Mystics & Contactees*, published by Illuminet Press in 1992. Find it if you can and read it! It speaks much on the religious dimension and how we have been manipulated by hidden forces from the earliest of times. John Keel wrote the introduction.

John Mack, second on the list, is a more recent proponent of this ultraterrestrial view. Mack appeared on a Fox TV program in 1995 called *Encounters: The Hidden Truth*, where he spoke about the abduction phenomenon and the genetic experiments that seem to be performed on the victims. He stated,

> "It's a preparation for the future in which another race of beings will exist in some dimension. Again, this . . . means we've got to open to dimensions that are not literally of this physical reality. We don't know in what dimension this joined race will exist, but it's as if it's a preparation for the end of the human experiment as we've known it."

Many researchers like Zecharia Sitchin and Dr. Arthur Horn are of the opinion that mankind is a genetic experiment that started in pre-history. I'm assuming that Dr. Mack is referring to this type of "experiment."

Mack is not as "hard line" on the ultraterrestrial theory as Keel and Vallee, leaving open the possibility that these aliens could come from somewhere in space before intruding into earth's neighboring dimensions. He went on to say,

> "The aliens come from some planet *or culture* which has destroyed itself. Their own stock is diminished, so they're coming here to replenish that. I mean, these are the great mysteries and I have all kinds of material about this from the experiencers that I've worked with." (italics mine)

Please note how Mack refuses to leave his statement at "some planet . . ." Adding "or culture" leaves it open to something that could be hidden right here on earth.

"Experiencer" is today's politically-correct version of "abductee." These people are sometimes told by aliens (or form conjectures of their own, based on first-hand experience) what the alien agenda really is.

Whatever the answers are, John Mack is searching for them. He is the first high-stature person from academia to step forward and give support and credence to the reality of UFOs and abductions. He is professor of psychiatry at The Cambridge Hospital at Harvard Medical School and is the author of *Abduction: Human Encounters with Aliens*. Because of his professional standing he has undergone much ridicule and criticism – mostly from peers who are not either open-minded enough to look into the problem, or brave enough to step forward as he has done.

Lastly, we cannot end without mentioning Dr. Gregory Little and his important book called *Grand Illusions*, published by White Buffalo Books in 1994. It would take volumes to get into Little's many fascinating theories and conclusions. In short, this is one of the best UFO books I've seen.

Much of Little's work centers around the electromagnetic energy spectrum (Keel's "superspectrum"), and is the perfect more modern update to Keel's incredible work from the 1970's.

Little also includes important work on the human mind and how it works in relation to strange phenomenon. He covers C.G. Jung's theory of mankind's "collective unconscious" – something we tap into, collectively, to generate our underlying thought structures. These thought structures form our deepest beliefs and manifest themselves as archetypes – symbols which we understand unconsciously better than consciously.

This unconscious world surfaces to us on occasion, and provides our best link to the usually untapped areas of the superspectrum. Understanding archetypes (as much as we consciously can) brings us closer to understanding the mythological stories from the past and strange modern occurrences of the present (which could be creating the mythologies of tomorrow).

These other dimensions, containing archetypal creatures found in the world's past mythologies, probably contain all of the modern aliens and UFOs that occasionally "cross over" and intrude on us.

Third Dimensional Limitations of Human Perception

One of these intruders seems to include Bigfoot. In China in 1995 a 3 month, extensive, high-tech search was conducted for Bigfoot in its most commonly sighted area – yet nothing, absolutely *nothing*, was found or seen. When these creatures are otherwise sighted, however, the smell of sulfur or rotten eggs permeates the air. Astute researchers into dimensional cross-over have noticed this as a common feature with creatures making such a journey. Red, glowing eyes is another one (found also in "Mothman," "The Jersey Devil," and other way-out creatures that vanish into thin air). Is Bigfoot such a creature? Ask the witnesses who report them with red, glowing eyes. The lack of physical evidence in other parts of the world where people have carefully searched for such creatures seems to point to this other-dimensional exit as the answer.

Dr. Little gets into describing the Vision Quest ritual of Native Americans, where little people are encountered. These little people fit the exact description we give to the grays that are associated with UFOs. Except with the Native American's tales, there are no UFOs. As Vallee would explain it, we white folks see more grays in UFOs because that is what we somehow expect to see, coming from a technically-based culture. These archetypal energies manifest themselves in a way to match our social outlook. Maybe this is done to keep us "comfortable" with their presence, to some degree, or maybe we are not able to observe them at all unless they appear within our "conscious framework" in some special way.

For instance, certain Indian tribes were shown photographs of themselves for the very first time, yet could not see themselves when given the prints! The different shadings of black and white meant nothing to them, and many natives turned the pictures over and stared at the blank white sides. Nothing in their conscious framework tipped them off as to what to look for.

Another example is with the true story of Magellan's ships arriving on an island in the Pacific. The natives had never seen ships before. A foreign guide stood with these natives on the shore, trying to point out the ships to them, which were clearly on the horizon, but the concept of a "ship" did not exist to them. None of the natives could see what was in plain view! Only after much explaining did the concept sink in and the ships were suddenly seen.

When it comes to alien beings and other dimensions, we are much like these native peoples. In order to experience something totally new and completely alien, our unconscious mind must pass along to the conscious mind a dim concept of it *first*, before the conscious mind will allow the eyes to function along *with the new concept* in order to recognize the image.

This is the key to these other-dimensional entities and their control over us. This is how they manifest themselves (from out of the collective unconscious) in ways that match our cultural expectations. They want to be seen. They want to be noticed. *But only in this subtle way.* Think about why. Once we catch on as to how the mind and other dimensions work, then we will open to the larger mysteries being withheld.

With each passing day, we get closer to this theory being verified. Whitley Strieber, in his 1995 book *Breakthrough*, states that he saw his first "visitor" as a kind of mother goddess figure. When he changed his conception of them to being an outgrowth of Celtic fairy mythology, then the visitors suddenly took on that appearance. Strieber says, "What changes is not what we see, but how they appear to us."

He goes on to say that this could account for our cultural view of seeing them as both angels and demons, based on strong Christian expectations. These beings somehow have a profound but also subtle effect on our consciousness.

It seems our biggest challenge in confronting alien life forms lies within our own minds. Our most intelligent scientists still refuse to accept that "they" are here. They would rather spend millions of dollars pointing SETI radio dishes into outer space, assuming that advanced life forms would choose to communicate in such a limited and primitive way. Terence McKenna put it well by saying,

> "To search expectantly for a radio signal from an extraterrestrial source is probably as culture-bound a presumption as to search the galaxy for a good Italian restaurant."

In other words, good luck.

If we can learn to view alien life forms with an open mind, we might then be able to see them as they really are. In the meantime, these creatures will continue to feed off our fears and expectations, causing us to view them inaccurately as they manifest in our world. If we can put a stop to this manipulation of our minds, individually and collectively, then we will have the key. We could then begin to expose the biggest con game this earth has ever known.

Exposing the Truth

How do we put a stop to this? I believe it must be a collective effort, based on what is known about the human mind and the archetypal world. If all people who 1) are experiencing the abduction phenomenon and 2) who are even remotely interested in UFOs, start *training* their minds to fully expect to confront entities who will reveal the truth of their actions and cooperate with our requests for information (instead of misinforming, terrifying, and genetically testing us against our will), then maybe it will happen. These hidden manipulations they impose on us are manipulations of the mind, first and foremost, then they do what they will with our bodies. A strong change in our thinking is necessary and could force a change in these hidden manipulations.

Being successful is a huge challenge, however. These entities always communicate with us through telepathic means. They get *right inside our heads!* We currently have no control over this subtle, yet powerful, intrusion. People hear alien "voices" in their heads when in their presence, and anything thought by us is perceived by these beings as clearly as we can hear. This is a very powerful control method and extremely invasive.

When abductees are returned, their memories are purposely "covered over" by these entities so that nothing is remembered unless deep hypnosis is used to recover the truth. The minds of these creatures are extremely strong and people often say it seemed as though the creature was "staring right through them," or had a "hypnotic power" over them.

So our training must be rigorous. Pre-hypnosis as opposed to post-hypnosis is an idea of mine that I have not heard elsewhere. If you know you are having encounters, do some preparation with a hypnotist *first*, instead of waiting to do all the depth work later. Maybe there is a way to program ourselves with barriers that these beings cannot get around so easily, if at all. We need to abolish our fears of these beings, both conscious and unconscious fears, so they cannot be used against us.

It seems only natural to fear creatures from the unknown – in fact, it may be an involuntary, instinctual fear that we have little or no control over. Let us work with qualified hypnotherapists to construct a program or programs that can help us.

Working alone, through meditation techniques, can also be a benefit. When in a deep meditation, it might be useful to implant a "no fear" message that will kick in should you ever encounter something that is other than human.

A "power" message under similar circumstances could either relieve you of such a visit or help you to gain useful information. Whatever feels comfortable to you should be used in preparation.

Many will read this and not act. Virtually all who read this have not prepared their minds for an alien encounter in any rigorous way. Why is that? Most wish to have such encounters because of our curious natures, yet have done nothing – *noth-ing* to prepare for such a thing.

Is it because we don't think it could happen to us? These things only happen to other people. Right?

It has been estimated by Bud Hopkins, among others, that people who have been abducted could number in the millions. Think about it. Our minds are like putty to them. We are so far behind, we have no idea how easily we can be manipulated. And should we ever discover it is true, we will deny it because of our egos! Our conscious minds (egos) are dominant and always refuse to acknowledge anything intruding from the unconscious areas. Social standards work the same way, and are usually more brutal.

For example, when Galileo discovered that the Earth was not the center of the universe it was the truth, but he was forced to recant. He knew that he was absolutely right, but became real humble in the face of death as an alternative. No one wants to hear the truth if it takes away from us being the all-powerful center of anything.

So if these entities are here, and have been here with us since the beginning, we are up against two barriers. The first is that they have reason to protect themselves and continue to hide. The second is our own inability to notice them, and then actually accept the fact, *really* accept the fact, that they are here. These are immense barriers, with staggering implications. But someday the truth will be known. We are being conditioned for it, as the opening of this work explained.

There is a world of wonder and information still yet undiscovered. Once we break through the scary part, the shocking part, things will open up for humanity. That is how it always works. Anything newly explored is frightening – because it is unknown. Once that barrier is crossed, and we begin to learn more about other dimensions and the true ways of the universe, mankind will burst forth and blossom in new ways, on a new spiritual level.

CHAPTER FIVE

IS RELIGION HARMFUL?
EXPLORING THE IMPACT OF RELIGION IN A MODERN AGE

JACK BARRANGER

Opening Statement: The Author's Background and Qualifications

I am qualified in this area for a number of reasons. First, I have a theological degree from Gordon-Conwell Theological Institute – a rock solid, Bible believing fundamentalist Christian seminary. I have spent much of my life as a leader of Christian groups ranging from Young Life to four different youth fellowship groups. In addition to my voluminous reading in seminary, I have also read deeply in the areas of sociology, anthropology, philosophy, history, and physics. With my minimal exposure to other religions in seminary, I have followed through on my own and read most of the holy books of the other world religions.

The more I read about Buddhism and quantum physics, the more I am amazed at how close the Bo tree revelations of Gautama Siddhartha and the latest discoveries of physics are linked. The more I read about archeological discoveries, the more I realize that the gods and heroes mentioned in mythology are actually historical characters. I increasingly realize the absurdity of claiming that Jehovah and Moses were real life people, but Zeus and Odysseus were simply figments of a blind poet's imagination. Further study of recently discovered ancient epics begs us to consider that Zeus, Jehovah, and Enlil (the main god of the Sumerians) were probably all the same entity.

However, I have done much more than spend long hours reading scholastic texts. My experience with youth groups was quite edifying. During many of the retreats I attended with young people, I saw lives transformed. I actually contributed to having young people go forward to receive Christ during a final night altar call. Into the wee hours of the morning, I talked with young people about why they should make God and Jesus the center of their lives. I firmly believed – at that time – that this was my holy mission, a calling from the Lord himself. In solitude I prayed for errant young souls, fully confident that the answer to their problems lay in putting God or Jesus first in their lives.

I still tremble in a good way as I remember 90 young

Does religion offer genuine spiritual truth? Religious systems are often damaging, misleading copies of something much higher.

voices singing some rousing hymn or a quiet folk tune such as "Blowing in the Wind." I was a believer then, and I was convinced that I could serve God best by helping the young people I loved become better believers – or first time believers. Something in me stirred deeply as I saw lives transformed and "souls on fire for the Lord."

While I am no longer a "believer," I spent more than half of my life as a fervent believer. I spent two years in seminary preparing to preach the gospel. I have read the archeological, philosophical, and anthropological research of the past twenty years. After much research and increasing anguish in my soul, I have come to the conclusion that we have not been told the truth about our religious origins. We have selected the comfortable and edifying, and ignored the terrible and horrifying. Even worse, we have ignored the evidence of archeological discoveries and the resultant writings they produced. By this selective unawareness, we prevent ourselves from being able to answer some very important questions:

What was the real reason for the creation of religion?

Were the creators of our religion divine?

Did the creators of our religions really care about us?

While I will answer the (above) three questions briefly, a much more thorough discussion of these questions can be found in my book *Past Shock: The Origin of Religion and Its Impact upon the Human Soul* (a sample chapter is found earlier in this book). I intend in this material to discuss and answer three other equally import questions:

• Is religion harmful to the human soul?

• Is an even greater form of religion possible?

• Is there one true religion?

A Brief History of Religion

If you are not familiar with the material of Zecharia Sitchin, the Book Tree, or The Prometheus Project, you might find the following material hard to digest. As hard as the material is to digest, it can be supported with solid evidence much more than what most religious people have become comfortable with. I must be honest with you and tell you that if I had read my own material ten years ago, I would have found it very hard to believe. I urge you to listen with an open mind.

Twelve thousand years ago a group of very advanced beings created the human race as a worker race. They were on the point of mutiny and decided that interfering with the evolution of beings on this planet was a better idea than having a mutiny among their workers. Thus, they created humanity as a worker force – a genetic cross between Neanderthal Man and themselves. However, we did not turn out like they had planned. We were too intelligent, too curious, and too rebellious – especially when it came to doing menial work. The genetic experimentation continued. However, a form of conditioning was added. A form of conditioning which would insure that we would work without complaint, fight their wars, and provide them adulation as gods. This condition turned out to be the first experience of organized religion.

Thus, the creation of religion was a tool to keep the newly created humans obedient and rigorously disciplined to accomplish the aims of those who created the religions.

Were the creators of religion divine? No. They simply told us they were divine, and we were not yet advanced enough to see through their lies. The newly created humans were willing to work harder for what they thought were divine beings. Sadly, being technologically advanced does not guarantee being spiritually advanced.

Did the creators of our religions really care about us? That depends on your viewpoint. They saw us as valuable to the degree that we were able to relieve them of work they didn't want to do. They saw us as quite valuable when we would fight wars for them. And they must have seen us as quite entertaining when we worshipped them or played games for them. (The Greek Olympics were originally created as an entertainment for the gods on Mount Olympus.)

A common thread that runs through all the answers to these three questions is that religion was created to manipulate and motivate us. The focus was not on our spiritual growth as much as it was getting us to do what they wanted.

With this knowledge as a foundation, it is the next three questions we shall address one by one, and with greater depth.

Is Religion Harmful to the Human Soul?

Yes, much more than we are willing to admit to ourselves. The main harm which religion does is substitute belief for spiritual experience. This is not to say that religion is against spiritual experience; however, the focus of most religions is getting their followers to believe certain tenets of their religion. What is most ironic about this is that most of the great world religions' founders were nowhere near as concerned about belief as their eventual followers.

Jesus, Mohammed, and Buddha would probably be shocked to see what was happening with the religions they are said to have founded. Jesus would probably wince in horror seeing that some young girl was missing a dance because her religion deemed it sinful. Mohammed would most likely cringe in disbelief if he saw all the Jihad's (holy wars) which have been spawned in his name. Buddha probably would have no interest in all the pomp and circumstance linked to the rituals done in his name. He probably would cry about the facts that young monks have to memorize 64,000 aphorisms to be deemed worthy of being a Buddhist monk.

In the Christian religion so many important facets are linked to the human experience. It becomes difficult to determine whether the experience is coming from a deep rooted archetypal conditioning or whether the experience is a genuine spiritual experience. When one hears Bach's magnificent *B Minor Mass* or Handel's *Messiah,* is the person moved by God or good music . . . or both? Yet another question must be considered. If we are deeply moved by a great piece of religious classical music or a simple hymn tune, couldn't it be possible that we are reinforcing the negative conditioning inflicted upon us thousands of years ago?

I passionately love Handel's oratorio *Israel in Egypt.* Its choruses are stirring musical masterpieces proclaiming the victory of Jehovah and the Israelites over the forces of Pharaoh. As a young teenager this deepened my Christian faith and further "convinced" me that Jehovah was indeed the true God. Now I realize that this wonderful music only more deeply etched my experience as a believer and blocked my growth as a soul. I now realize that the composer Handel was much greater than the Jehovah he was celebrating. No one among those pretender gods (entities who lied to us by telling us that they were God) could have written something as magnificent as Handel's *Israel in Egypt.*

They were technologically advanced far beyond what we are now. However, in matters of the soul they were cretins. Not one of them could have written a Wordsworth sonnet. None of them could have sculpted Michelangelo's David. (Most of the great sculptures of the world were all done by humans honoring the gods.) No pretender god could have even come close to composing something as magnificent as Beethoven's *Ninth Symphony.*

Beethoven has brought us more closely aligned with joy than any of the pretender gods did with their created religions. In one of the greatest experiences of cosmic irony, a group of "gods" actually created something artistically greater than themselves – us. The inspiration Beethoven was tapping into was something higher than Jehovah – Beethoven was most likely tapping into the true God, what the-ologian Paul Tillich referred to as "the God beyond God." And this brings us to a question much more important than *Is religion harmful to the soul?* That question to be considered is:

Is religion blocking us from experiencing the true God?

Obviously, yes, and we'll elaborate on that soon.

Is a Greater Form of Religion Possible?

The answer is also yes. However, I immediately pose another question:

Is a good form of religion even possible?

Let's examine this. A better form of religion is definitely possible; however, the better question to ask is "Is it a good idea?" If religion is a reinforcement of condi-tioning, it is not a good idea. If religion is something which frees the human expe-rience to experience the true God, then – despite how rare this might be – it is a good idea. Malcolm Muggeridge in *Jesus Rediscovered* claimed that the closer a person came to God, the more alienated he felt from his religion. God – the true God – has a habit of doing that to people despite the wailing consternations of reli-gious leaders. The problem with organized religion is that it is like a T.V. dinner: what's inside the box is never as good as the picture on the box. Organized religion promises God and delivers conditioning to belief structures. It's a losing proposi-tion, no matter how good it makes some people feel.

Finding the true God can happen much more easily outside of structured reli-gion. The problem is that people have become so addicted to the ritual and condi-tioned belief, that leaving their religion causes both guilt and withdrawal pains. Add to this some religious structures which will deem your withdrawal – and even your liberation – as "falling away" or sinful, and the experience of the "God beyond God" becomes even more difficult.

Just as the ancient religions had priests to tell people what to think and what "God hath ordained," we Americans have ministers, priests, and rabbis. Ninety per cent of these people I have met – and I have met hundreds – are very good people. Unlike the ancient creators of our religions, many do not want to harm you or manipulate you. However, they do want to tell you what to believe, and in this they are unwittingly doing spiritual harm. Many times I was positively influenced by a youth minister who helped me by caring about me as a person, yet harmed me by keeping me locked into a rigid belief system that too often blocked spiritual expe-rience. I was so beguiled by the goodness of the person that I was incapable of exploring whether the system had value.

So where does a young person get his morality? This is a good question and a very tough answer. The religion of Taoism claims that morality pushed to excess creates immorality (*Tao Te Ching*). Buddhism explores a middle path between the extremes of life codes. Christianity is much more rigid (despite the Christian liber-ty explained in Romans 14). And this very rigidity blocks the direct experience of God.

The way that many spiritual leaders and gurus of the world's great religions act, one would swear that there was no God available for help. Many in the Islamic faith feel that they have to fight holy wars in order to be true to their faith; while they give lip service to Allah, they act as if they have to get it done themselves. Christians are not free of this mentality. While they claim the power of the Holy Spirit, many act as if the Holy Spirit had no power at all. They spend great money for church lighting and sound systems to insure that the experience is magnificent – even if it isn't Godly.

Those who experience God directly do not have the need of a belief system. In fact, after such an experience, any belief system is considered irrelevant. The Holy Spirit is not locked into such a sorority mentality that he/she/it will perform only for members in the fold. All the great religious texts reveal that this isn't the case. God – the "God beyond God" – is available for all. The great tragedy is that most religious people simply aren't interested. Their interest lies mainly in a God who fits comfortably into their limited paradigm. If they experienced the true God, those paradigms would shatter. And that can be a very frightening experience for many people. Meanwhile, the "God" of organized religion continues to be a warrior demanding a battle for the faith and the embracing of an ancient belief system which was as false then as it is now.

Is there One True Religion?

No! A thousand times no! This is one of the most soul-depleting beliefs ever inflicted upon humanity. While this is not worthy of the true God, it is typical of religions founded in the name of the ancient beings who claimed to be God. Only pretenders to divinity could inflict such a demand on an "inferior" species.

The true God is neither petty not insecure. However, one who pretends is always insecure in the reality that they might be found out. The true God does not fear being found out; he probably would like just to be found. Standing between the human experience and the true God lies a mighty conditioning so powerful that finding this true God becomes quite difficult. Humans after thousands of years of ancient conditioning find themselves more comfortable continuing this conditioning than they do looking for the truth. What is conditioning is comfortable and predictable. Unfortunately, it is not true.

What ironically blocks our experiencing the true God is our obsession to be a part of the true religion. Like the college student who wants to be in the best fraternity, so do humans want to feel the exclusivity of belonging to the true religion. These "true religions" will go to great lengths to prove their point. Roman Catholics no longer burn people at the stake for heretical beliefs, but it was done. Many Protestant sects (like the Catholics) persecuted normal women as "witches" in the Middle Ages. They both believe that if a person lives a good life according to their faith, they will find eternal rest. The interpretation of this could sometimes turn cruel, vicious, and very unfair, all in the name of God. The many facets of the modern fundamentalist Christian experience continue to warn about dancing, dream analysis, meditation, and the "evil" umbrella of the New Age movement. It is not a matter of whether organized religion has insane and sane levels; it is, however, more about the pathetically few adherents of any religion who are willing to look at what happened thousands of years ago which insanely continues to live on in modern religion.

No, there is no true man-made religion. There is no true religion because all religions are lost in rituals and beliefs which inhibit rather than enhance the spiritual experience. Ritual insures repetition, and repetition insures the predictable. This is not fertile ground for the Holy Spirit to operate. Because God is a creator on the spiritual level, He (She, It) logically would want his creations to be co-creators with Him (Her, It). A God who creates souls, various dimensions of reality, and perhaps even the Universe would not want His subjects going through endless rituals and incessantly praising His name. He would not elect – to the exclusion of others – a small tribe in the Middle East or a group of only one color in Africa. And He certainly would not determine that there was only one religion by which any seeker could embrace Him. He would never sink to the mentality that Beta Pi's are in but Kappa Sigmas are going to burn. He would not experience anger if a Sigma Chi married one of the forbidden Chi Omega's. The true God – Tillich's "God beyond God" – does not involve Himself in such a mentality.

This mentality exists because we voluntarily continue to brainwash ourselves with lies that we would swear to God were true. We should not blame ourselves for this because we were highly conditioned to do it. These beliefs were etched into us in great terror, and they remain at the cellular level. We were raped by pretenders, and thousands years later we are still worshipping those who raped us.

This is the greatest harm of religion – the fact that we voluntarily keep ourselves in hell when heaven lies deep within us. Religion does great harm when it continues the conditioning of the belief that what happens to us after we die is more important than what happens to us now. However, one of the greatest harms of religion is that it keeps alive a woeful conditioning that aids people in feeling good when they continue their slave ways. Eruptions of guilt are felt just at the point when one begins walking on the path to spiritual liberation. The harm of religion is that it has kept people worshipping their chains and praising the entities that chained their souls.

What is the harm of religion? It hinders the experience of God.

Yet, if God is saying "Embrace me: I can take you to higher levels," many will reply, "No thanks. I'm comfortable with what I've got. It may not give me power, but it sure does give me certainty."

Once again, God says "I am deep within you. Embrace me there." The reply this time is "Get thee behind me, Satan. I don't listen to that New Age nonsense."

One more time God says, "I want to set you free," and the reply is, "Sorry, in my religion the only way you can truly be free is to be a slave to God."

These souls are riding round and round on a merry-go-round reaching for the brass ring. Every once in a while someone catches one of the brass rings and edifies the masses giving rousing testimony to the masses. This inspires more to get on the merry-go-round and even more fervently lunge for the brass ring. Round and round they go chanting, singing, shouting slogans, and making a "joyful" noise. What none of them understands is that going for the brass ring is not the name of the game.

The name of game is getting off the merry-go-round.

Questions and Answers

Don't you think it would be cruel to take a person's religion away from them? Some people have spent their whole lives nurturing a belief system.

I agree with you. I would never – even if I had the power – take away a person's belief system. Some people get great pleasure in rattling people's cages concerning their religion.

But aren't you rattling people's cages in what you are saying here?

You have voluntarily read *Is Religion Harmful?* You're an adult, and I assume you have good powers of discernment. If you were looking for religious edification, you certainly were aware that this would not be the place.

How do we stop the harm that religion is doing? Do you have any suggestions?

At this point in time, I'm not even sure that it's a good idea to attempt to do this. Many good books are written on the subject, and this movement has been going on for some time. A century ago a man named Robert Ingersoll was packing the houses lecturing on this same theme. However, he was probably a man long before his time. He did not have the benefit of the ancient writings and archeological writings which we have now.

So you think we're going to experience a revival – or perhaps even a de-revival?

Now there's an interesting concept. Rather than a de-revival, I think we are closer to seeing a flower that is going to bloom. The Protestant Reformation didn't really begin with Martin Luther in Germany. It started in the late 1300's with John Hus and Jerome of Prague – and a military leader named general Zitzka. All they wanted was to be able the read the Bible in Czech – their own language. Each of these men died for this cause – along with many other brave souls. The consensus reality was that this attempt at reformation was short lived and futile. Yet Martin Luther himself said, "This Reformation was bought by the blood of John (Hus) and Jerome. " They sowed seeds which grew 130 years later in Germany.

I believe that Robert Ingersoll – and others like him – sowed seeds a century ago, and they are now beginning to sprout. I believe that this will eventually move on its own power.

How can you say that? Organized religion is stronger than ever. Cults are on the rise. The Christian Right seems to be gaining power.

I know that this is going to sound naive, but some wonderful things are starting to happen – things that are happening on their own. Jordan Maxwell – a very good friend of mine – could barely muster an audience talking about ancient religious conspiracies. Now how fills the lecture halls. People's hunger for an alternative view is increasing exponentially.

He is one of the writers of a book called *The Book Your Church Doesn't Want You to Read.* This is an excellent book by writers like Alan Snow, Jordan Maxwell, and Steve Allen – more than forty writers (including Robert Ingersoll) who want to inform you about what you have not been told about our religious past and our religious present.

Tim Leedom, the editor of the book, gave a lecture to a group of Protestant ministers and was experiencing fear and trepidation. He knew these were good people and that he wasn't going to be lynched, but he was concerned that his material would alienate them.

Not so. They were angry – but neither at Tim nor his book. They were angry that they had never been told anything about the real history during their theological education.

What is it in this supposedly lurid past that could rattle and shake up a group of ministers?

Do you have a spare three days?

Seriously, this is a very deep issue – and quite frankly not very pleasant. I have additional material to sell which covers some of that. My book *Past Shock* explains what happened thousands of years ago along these lines. Succinctly put – if anyone can even put this material succinctly – what happened thousands of years ago was not pretty. Jehovah, who claimed that he created the heavens and the earth, was not a very nice entity. He wasn't anything close to being God. Instead, he was a mentally deranged warlord who told the Israelites that he was God and that he had chosen them for a special mission.

Some mission. This mission involved marching around the hot desert with many starving to death. When people complained that they were hungry, Jehovah responded with poisonous snakes, beatings, and death sentences. He demanded that a man be stoned to death because he was picking up sticks on the Sabbath. He told his own that they would have to eat their own excrement if they didn't do as they were told. This is an entity who expressed great joy when one of his human charges impaled one of his fellow humans because this "errant soul" dared to work on the Sabbath. This was not a compassionate all-loving God. This was a psychically deranged warlord.

I've heard you lecture before and you have claimed that you should look for the good in even the worst people. Could you possibly say anything good about Jehovah?

I'm sorry I'm laughing. Shoot, this is a real stretch. Yeah, I remember something from my seminary days. Jehovah had come to one of the minor prophets and claimed that he was going to destroy Israel. (In the past Jehovah not only made the threat to destroy Israel but he also followed through on those threats.) However, this time, he came back a couple of days later and said, "I cannot destroy Israel."

Before any of you go into spasms of tears from being so moved, I must tell you that many Bible scholars feel that there were actually four Jehovah's. They have figured this out by studying the linguistic structures of their spoken words. Jehovah – or Yahweh as the scholars like to call him – was an epithet. Not an epithet like "damn" or "hell" but more like a given name. This last Jehovah was probably only neurotic. He actually showed some compassion.

But what about people like me who believe that Jehovah is indeed God?

I'm sorry that you believe that, but I can't judge you because I believed that for a period of time that is probably longer than you have been alive. My experience and research tells me that this is a counterproductive belief. However, I believed that because of my conditioning. As a very young boy, I read the Bible on my own. I remember the crisis I had when I read the story about a group of Israelites carrying the Ark of the Covenant. As it was about to tip over, Uzzah – one of the Israelites – ran up and attempted to keep it from falling over. According to the Biblical account, Uzzah was struck dead by Jehovah.

As a young boy I could not understand how a loving God would strike dead a man who was trying to help God. So I discussed this with my parents, and they said that some things about God we just can't understand. I then asked my minister, and he said that God had given very strict orders that no one touch the Ark of the Covenant and went on to say that God's rules had to be followed. He tops it off with the old saying that God in his infinite wisdom knew what he was doing.

Then, I go see the movie *David and Bathsheba.* Now on the big screen I get to watch Uzzah struck dead by the wrath of God. But to complicate things further, the movie ends with Gregory Peck as David intentionally touching the Ark and *not* being struck dead. So now we have David, a flagrant adulterer, not being struck dead and Uzzah, someone who was trying help, being zapped by an angry Jehovah.

I had to go back to the Bible to find that David didn't really touch the Ark. However, at that tender young age there was no one to tell me that this was not God but instead "gods" who had no spiritual value at all at this point in time. No one was around to tell me that Uzzah was probably electrocuted – as anyone would have been had they touched an electrified Ark.

This is a roundabout way of answering the question, but it points out that I was conditioned from a very young age to believe that Jehovah was God. I was conditioned by very well meaning parents who themselves had been conditioned at a very young age by their well meaning parents. So it was with their parents. We believe that Jehovah was God because of conditioning that has been going on for thousands of years. However, once one begins examining the evidence, one finds the evidence for Jehovah being God just doesn't hold up. We are so well programmed that we feel guilty if we feel anything different. However, feeling something different is the only way to go. Jehovah is not God – he never was.

Do you think I get joy out of saying that? My mouth goes dry every time I make a statement like that. I feel almost like a dog who's crapped on the rug. I remember coming home one day and being shocked that my dog Sappho didn't run up to greet me. I knew there was no way my wife could have gotten home first, so this appeared very strange. Then I saw it: Sappho had taken a very big dump on the rug. Like angry Jehovah, I called out to Sappho with a very deep voice – you know like Jehovah did after Adam and Eve did their no-no. I knew Sappho was in the house. After fifteen minutes of searching, I found a trembling Sappho underneath some clothes in the closet. At that moment I realized that I had forgotten to let Sappho out to attend to nature. Now I was looking at a guilt-ridden dog that had done nothing wrong,

I hugged her, stroked her, and probably over-dosed her with Milk Bones, and she still felt guilty. The difference between me and Jehovah is that Jehovah would have just whomped her and screamed "Bad dog!" I feel that whoever we worship as God should be much more compassionate than Jehovah – and certainly more compassionate than me.

If the true God is so compassionate, why didn't He intervene when Jehovah was doing all these nasty things?

Well, Joe, God in His infinite wisdom knew what he was . . . No seriously, I honestly don't know the answer to that one. If I had had the power of Jehovah and his ilk, I would have tried to stop it. We do have accounts of people who did try to make a difference. In the *Atra Hasis* – a Sumerian epic that predates the Bible and is the established foundation for the first chapters of Genesis, Enki (the brother of Enlil) knows that a flood is coming. Enlil – whom many historians think was Jehovah – wants all of the human race to conveniently drown. You know – the mass aqua solution for disposing of the pain-in the-butt species. However, Enki – Enlil's brother – warns Utnapishtim that a flood is coming and instructs him how to build an ark. Utnapishtim – damn that's a rough one. No wonder they changed his name to Noah. Anyhow, Enki warns what's-his-face so that some of humanity can be saved.

This is where it gets very interesting. According to the *Atra Hasis,* all of the Anunnaki (the gods) are hovering above watching millions of humans frantically drowning. Many of them begin weeping. Finally. Enlil/Jehovah begins weeping. At that point brother Enki says, "Guess what I did?"

You would think that Enlil would have been possessed with joy hearing that some of their created worker humans had been saved. However, he went into a violent rage and wouldn't talk to Enki for weeks. The point here is that some of the gods did care – they did want to help despite the fact that they were exploiting us.

William Bramley in his groundbreaking book *The Gods of Eden* tells of a group called The Brotherhood of the Serpent which was concerned about the spiritual development of this newly formed human race. They secretly gave spiritual instruction to the human race and told them flat out that the gods were not God. From this you can get a better perspective of the Garden of Eden incident. This brings a whole new light to Prometheus' decision to steal fire from the gods and give it to humanity. This Brotherhood of the Serpent was not the devil or anything evil; this was a group of gods who were sick and tired of the harm that the religion these gods had created was doing to people. That harm is still going on today. However, this time we don't have any outlaw gods to help us. We're on our own.

You said earlier that . . . I think you used the expression "perhaps God creat -ed the Universe." If God didn't create the Universe, who did?

Many views exist on this. The Christian Gnostics believe that an inferior god created the Universe. They referred to this entity as the Crazy Creator God. The formal name is the Demiurge. This Crazy Creator/Demiurge started a creation in the world of matter. The true God is a God of spirit and would not create in the world of matter because this was a very dense vibration which was considered the "vibration of illusion." However, this Crazy Creator God created in this world of illusion.

And here we are.

This is one of the greatest harms of religion – believing that God would create in the world of illusion. I am amazed how people rape their minds and souls by claiming that disease, cobra snakes, hurricanes, cockroaches, and a whole bunch of goodies are related to God. A friend of mine from Bolivia told me that there is this insect which flies into your ear and immediately burrows its way to the area of your brain which controls your motor functions. In a matter of minutes you are rendered helpless. Then this cute little thing renders other parts of your brains useless until you die. Now all of this makes more sense being created by a creator that is insane.

I just can't see a compassionate God creating such things as this. To project these horrors onto the true God is a travesty.

A Course in Miracles takes this a step further. It claims that we are the creators of the Universe. Now there's a really happy thought. At one point in the *Course in Miracles* the voice that dictated it – which some claim was Jesus – claims that if we knew what we did to ourselves in our own acts of creation that we would tremble in uncontrollable terror. I tremble in terror to think that anyone could think that God would create AIDS or any other disease. I can't believe that we refer to earthquakes and other natural disaster as "acts of God." Poor God, He just can't win.

But this, once again, is the manifestation of human minds raped by organized religion. As well intentioned as the majority of religions are, they still have their foundation in horrific events which the extreme majority of us don't even want to remember. I strongly urge you to remember. As we begin to remember, we can begin to understand how we evolved – or de-evolved – as a species. That point of remembrance is descending on us very quickly.

CHAPTER SIX

A CALL FOR HERESY
BRINGING CHOICE AND FREEDOM TO HUMANITY'S SPIRITUAL EXPERIENCE

JACK BARRANGER

He who believes in a system wears a blindfold.
—Robert Anton Wilson
Most people are prisoners of their own brains.
—Richard Bandler

Throughout history, the words "heretic" and "heresy" have received very bad press. In some circles these two words are used respectively with "evil one" and "evil." The words "heretic" and "heresy" can make such an emotional impact that some people will alter their very beliefs in order to avoid this label. Being called a heretic is something to be avoided. To engage in heresy is too often interpreted as meaning that one has "fallen away" or "departed from the true path."

This highly limited perception of heresy and heretics persists despite the fact that Jesus, Mohammed, Guatama Buddha, and virtually all "founders" of the world's religions were considered heretics in their own time. Buddha departed from the confining strains of his Hindu faith by claiming that our thoughts determined our reality. Jesus upset the Pharisees by daring to suggest that some of the Pharisees' laws were more limiting than spiritual. He also promoted unpopular ideas like loving your enemies and pursuing a lifestyle other than what one's parents had determined for their children.

Sadly, people use labels like heretic and heresy to manipulate people in the name of Jesus, Mohammed, and Buddha (as well as the core people of other world religions). This sets up a most interesting paradox: one is labeled a heretic when he *appears* to be departing from the statutes of his or her religion. However, careful scrutiny reveals that one is probably being called a heretic because he or she is blazing trails into an even deeper spiritual experience. Most are caught up in the chains of a religion which was inspired by an original heretic (who is now the established foundation for the religion).

For those who are confused with the idea of heresy, let's provide an example. John Hus was one of the first church leaders to suggest that people should be able to read the Bible in their own language (Czechoslovakian). However, the Church

fathers were *very* threatened by this. They wanted to be guardians of the "Holy Word" and did not want common people to be able to read the Bible for themselves. Therefore, they branded John Hus a heretic.

During long sessions at the Council of Constance (1416-1418), Hus gave more than thirty references from the scriptures themselves which suggested that what was considered the word of God should be read by the people. The leaders of the Council of

The Buddha and Jesus: Both were heretics during their lives

Constance all agreed with the scriptural validity of the references made by Hus. Despite this, John Hus was burned at the stake.

Why? Because the leaders determined that he was a heretic.

What Exactly Is a Heretic?

The stifling of the individual may well be the stifling of the God in man.

—Sri Aurobindo

We fear our highest possibilities. We are generally afraid to become that which we can glimpse in our most perfect moments, under condi-tions of great courage. We enjoy and even thrill to the godlike possi-bilities we see in ourselves and in such peak moments. And yet we simultaneously shiver with weakness, awe, and fear before those very same possibilities.

—Abraham Maslow

The word "heretic" comes from the Greek simply meaning "one who chooses." A heretic is one who chooses what he will believe – and eventually moves to a level of mental freedom where he no longer needs beliefs to dominate his spiritual expe-rience. In no way is a person a heretic (the old negative form) if she chooses to believe something other than what she has been taught by her culture, society, or church. However, a person is a heretic (the good form) if she chooses beliefs other than what she has been taught. In essence, she is saying, "I am choosing a new level of experience because my old experience is neither satisfying or meaningful."

In this context the a person is not a heretic because he believes something dif-ferent from what is considered "the truth" or "the only way." Instead, a person becomes a heretic when he begins making choices for himself based on his experi-ence and spiritual exploration. This means that not only is heresy a good idea, it also means that heresy is essential in the spiritual quest of each individual human being.

If a heretic is one who chooses, then heresy is the act of choice. Heresy is not evil. Nor is it something that is a part of falling away from the truth. Actually, heresy is an essential part of marching toward the truth. Heresy is an indication that a person is ready to begin giving up his conditioned beliefs and is ready to choose new ways of perception based on his experiences and his exploration.

A Call for Heresy

The lover is a psycho-spiritual outlaw, free of all cultural taboos, yet profoundly responsible.

—Robert A. Masters from *The Way of the Lover*

The world does not need people who are faithful to the doctrines of the faith which they are expected to maintain and nurture. Instead, the world needs people who will move from their very safe comfort zones and actively pursue heresy. Despite all the noises made about how great the religious experience is, the reli-gious experience actually remains a force for the *conditioning of the mind* rather than *the release of the mind*. Thus, spiritual growth and mental development require that a person move from conditioned beliefs and attitudes and begin the process of making saner choices.

Thus, this is a call for heresy. It is a plea for people to break free from the chains of their religious conditioning and seek a path based on experience rather than dogma or replayed archetypes. (The Swiss psychiatrist Carl Gustav Jung claimed that archetypes are mental sets deep within us which make a powerful impact upon our lives. These are very old and have been influencing us for thousands of years.)

If Buddha could see the ritual and mental demands placed on people in the Buddhist faith today, he would probably weep. Here is a religious leader who made a point of stilling and emptying his mind. Yet, if he were here today, he would find the monks of his faith engaging in raping minds with the expectation of Herculean feats of memory and rigid ritual. (I am aware that much of this ritual has the intention of emptying, stilling, or liberating the mind; however, much of the original purpose has been lost in the development of dogma and religion.)

If Jesus Christ could see the religious "litigation" which has blossomed in his name, he might be tempted to step forward and say, "I don't remember saying that dancing was sinful." He also might say, "In addition to urging that an adulteress sin no more, I also did not judge her. I suggest that you do the same." To people who limit themselves and somehow convince themselves that this highly limited life is spiritual, Jesus might say, "I have come that you might have life and have it more abundantly." (John 10:10)

Jesus was not only a heretic in his time, but also called people to choose a better way (in other words "to be a heretic"). The call for heresy is not something instituted by this writer as much as it has been by the spiritual trail-blazers of the past. They were "divine ass-kickers" who wanted people to move from their sleep to a new level of waking – moving up to better and more effective choices. The call for heresy is not something new; it is instead something which has been forgotten by people who have become so comfortable with their religious indoctrination that they fail to realize that their religion is supposed to "shake things up" and move them to even better choices.

Consider Being a Divine Heretic

Those who are asleep to their true nature cannot be trusted, for they are strangers to their integrity.

—Robert A. Masters

The tragedy with most religious doctrines is that they focus more on doctrine than spiritual experience. In one of those most ironic of intentions, the pursuit of the "right doctrine" actually prevents spiritual experience. The obsession for the "right beliefs" is an insurance policy against experiencing God. By limiting one's religious experience to one hour a week on a pre-established day, the poor Holy Spirit (or High Self) is strangled in what it can do.

The heretic is not limited to a pre-digested belief system. He also is not limited to a certain way of experiencing God. Nor is he stuck in the extremely naive idea that all spiritual experiences have to feel good or happen within his limited paradigm. Like the spiritual leader and writer Joel Goldsmith, the heretic says, "Let me experience the breadth of the spiritual experience and then make choices based on those experiences." The heretic does not choose in advance a pre-digested group of beliefs and then "demand" that his future experiences fall within those beliefs. Instead, he remains open to choose what he thinks might be the truth based on his own experiences with God, his Higher Self, the Holy Spirit, the Dynamic Ground, the Force, the God beyond God, Brahman, or any other spiritual force capable of leading one from sleep into a state of becoming awake.

Those Who Are Terrified of Heretics

Powerful churches, political parties, and vested financial interests... have a strong desire to program the rest of us into the particular "Real" universes which they find profitable, and to keep us from becoming self-programmers. They want to "take responsibility" for us, and they do not want us to "take responsibility" for ourselves.

—Robert Anton Wilson

Since the birth of religion, we have always had a "ruling priest class" which has stood ready to tell us what the true faith is and which beliefs are deemed acceptable. What has kept this ruling priest class alive are the millions of people who want to be told what the true way is and what to believe. They want their religion or faith to be like a TV dinner that simply needs to be slipped in the oven – with little thought or preparation necessary. Like the TV dinner, these religions or faiths are highly processed and almost totally lacking in any nourishment. They merely pander to the comfort of those who are terrified to choose. In other words, those who are terrified to be true heretics have chosen for themselves a falsely comfortable way of learning about and relating to God.

There's just one problem with all of this: God often has a hard time getting through the barriers of these processed religions. Because people demand that their religious experience happen within their limited paradigms, they set up very narrow ways of experiencing God, the Holy Spirit, and divine guidance which can come from within. (Jesus did say that the Kingdom of God was within us.)

Yet, people who break free from their cultural and religious conditioning are threatening to people who have chosen the conditioned religious approach. In fact, the closer the heretic moves toward experiencing God, the more the majority of people feel that this person is actually falling away from God. In a pompously paradoxical perversion, they pray that this heretical person will quickly return to the fold. Ironically, it is actually "the fold" which has prevented the emerging heretic from experiencing a closer relationship with God. Many a well meaning person will sit down with a person and – with the sincerest of intentions – urge a person to return to the old conditioned way of approaching God. The one urging the return assures the emerging heretic that the old way is best – even though that way no longer works (nor will it ever again work) for the emerging heretic.

That's why this "emerging" person must become a heretic: his past ways and conditioned responses no longer work. He needs to strike out and choose a better way. Despite the fact that he is upsetting parents, family members, and friends, he *must* leap into a space where he is free to make choices. If he does not have the freedom to make choices, his spiritual growth will be stunted, and he will only have "more of the same " for spiritual nourishment. In other words, his "return to the fold" practically insures that he will have little or no spiritual nourishment.

What he will get is merely the "satisfaction" of "knowing" that he is no longer a threat to the people in his fold. This is almost always a devastating price to pay on the spiritual quest.

Why the Heretical Path Is Essential

> When the walls are down, the world can expand. And that is the dif -
> ference between a world that could be a heaven and one that becomes
> a hell.
>
> —Deepak Chopra

The heretical path is essential because it is the only path with genuine choice. Other paths have pre-digested dogma and pre-selected beliefs as expectations. A person could have a genuine spiritual experience at a Billy Graham rally. However, instead of leaving the person's spiritual growth to the Holy Spirit, well meaning people guide this "new convert" into an extremely narrow range of things to do which center more on dogma than experience.

The "new convert" will be told that *only* her newly discovered path leads to eternal life. She will be told that she must study only the scriptures of this new found faith, that other scriptures are not true . . . perhaps even evil. She will be told that she must read those scriptures faithfully – thus brainwashing herself to accept the dogmas of this "new religion." If she encounters something in the Bible which suggests reincarnation, she will be told that entertaining such a notion is not spiritually correct. She will be shown "the way," and God help her if the Holy Spirit leads her in another direction.

The heretical path is essential because it keeps the human soul open for choices – choices which are more aligned with *holiness* and *divinity* than religion or doctrine. The heretical path keeps a person's options open so that divine guidance can flourish instead of being stifled "in the name of the Lord." It allows people to tap into and nurture the divine spark within instead of looking to a pre-established set of concepts which may have little to do with God or anything Godly. The heretical path allows humans to look within for God rather than depending on ancient or rigid rituals which have become overrated with the passing of time.

The heretical path allows a person to question beliefs which were instilled when a person was too young to question these beliefs. The idea of dying for one's faith can become so induced into a child's religious upbringing that the heretical idea of living one's life abundantly may actually take a back seat to a "dying for the Lord" mentality. A child may become so ingrained with the idea that God frowns on sex that she may not be able to enjoy sex once she is married. A teenager may be so obsessed with wanting to please the God of his conditioning that he may never explore better ways to experience the true God. A person who sincerely and truly wants to serve God may think the only effective ways to do this would be to become a pastoral minister or a missionary. The heretical path helps people get beyond these stultifying limitations and opens the way for a much more fulfilling and spiritual way of living.

Heresy is not something evil blocking the human experience. It is actually an essential part of the human experience.

Moving from Spiritual Slavery to Spiritual Liberation

I always thought that if something isn't working, that it might be an indication that it was time to do something else. If you know that something doesn't work, then anything else has a chance of working than more of the same thing.

—Richard Bandler

What exactly is spiritual slavery?

One is in a state of spiritual slavery when he or she feels that beliefs about the divine are more important than experiencing the divine. Most organized religions make the claim that a person must pursue certain spiritually correct beliefs. Many organized religions claim that a failure to possess the right beliefs will lead to eternal damnation or a separation from God. *Ironically, it is the possession of beliefs which contributes to a separation from God.* Beliefs are baggage that prevents genuine efforts to develop a relationship with the true God.

One is in a state of spiritual slavery when she feels that being right is more important than realizing truth. Most organized religions are much more concerned with telling someone what they consider to be the truth. They have it pre-digested so that exploration is "no longer necessary." Thus, instead of an exploration or a search for the truth, the twenty first century human merely needs to "find the correct TV dinner, plop it in the oven, and wait thirty minutes."

Being well conditioned and thoroughly brainwashed becomes much more important than becoming aware or becoming awake. In fact, most organized religions rarely provide experiences that increase awareness or move a person out of a state of being asleep. While most religion is well intended, it still is more aligned with brainwashing and conditioning. Because of this highly conditioned state of mind, heresy eventually becomes an essential part of spiritual liberation.

Heresy restores *choice* to the human experience. It says, "No matter what you have learned, you must allow your mind and your own personal experience to determine what works best for you."

The heretic realizes that God created each person as a unique human being and does not need his creations to fit into a cookie cutter type of religion. Each human is supplied with a brain-mind capable of grasping the distinction between *what works* in his spiritual experience and what is merely *acceptable.* Because humans are such "belonging oriented" creatures, too many would rather "belong to the 'right' religion" than determine for themselves what spiritual experiences work best in their lives. The idea that such a thing as a right religion represents a part of conditioning established more than 4,000 years ago. That idea was part of a conditioning process that was meant to manipulate humanity into a state of spiritual slavery. (This idea is discussed in much greater depth in *Past Shock: The Origin of Religion and Its Impact on the Human Soul*).

That conditioning process continues today in the form of organized religion, the concept that there could be only one right religion, and the counterproductive idea that one must pursue religious beliefs rather than spiritual experience. This conditioning process has created a highly refined form of spiritual slavery. Many people in this mind-set turn the spiritual quest into a deepening of spiritual slavery. They remain spiritual slaves because they have been very effectively conditioned to feel good about their brainwashing and other experiences, which only deepen their brainwashing. By continuing to insist that a right religion must exist, we continue to condition ourselves to embrace the lies which we were told more than 4,000 years ago by forces which used organized religion as a means of exploiting newly created humans instead of liberating them.

Therefore, this call for heresy is not a plea. It is a clarion call to wake up from the sleep-induced conditioning of the past. While that conditioning was very powerful, it is permanent only if it is constantly reinforced. While constant reinforcement is the choice of the majority of humans, it does not have to be your choice. Heresy allows you to stand outside of your conditioning and allow your own experiences to determine what works and what doesn't. (Interestingly enough, the word" ecstasy" originally meant "to stand outside of.") Heresy also allows you to bring choice back into your experience as a personal factor in creating your own spiritual liberation.

One begins the process of spiritual liberation by making the choice to pursue matters of genuine spiritual exploration instead of using personal energy to deepen the process of religious conditioning and brainwashing. This spiritual freedom comes from making choices based on personal revelation instead of acquired beliefs. Spiritual liberation will not happen until a person is free to make a choice. Sadly, few people are free to make choices until they are able to stand apart from the conditioning they had as a child.

While genuine spiritual liberation is always liberating, it isn't always initially edifying. We are very well conditioned creatures who desperately "need to believe." Thus, we will think that spiritual exploration and spiritual freedom lie in moving from one set of beliefs to yet another set of beliefs. This rarely works. It is more like changing the label on an empty bottle. Taking this analogy one step further, moving from one set of beliefs to yet another set of beliefs is more like pouring new wine into old wineskins.

Heresy and the Dark Night of the Soul

> *I have no intention of giving sanction to a new edi -
> tion of the old fiasco.*
>
> —Satprem

> *Whenever you get confused, you can get excited
> about the new understanding that awaits you.*
>
> —Sri Aurobindo

Too often, during the process of shifting from a belief-dominant paradigm to an experience-based paradigm, people encounter what the Hindu's refer to as a "dark night of the soul." During this "dark night of the soul," one feels a sense of emptiness. Nothing seems to work anymore. While this "dark night of the soul" may not feel good, it is almost always an indication that something good is happening. Instead of something appearing not to work, what happens is that the spiritual seeker wakes up to the fact that very little in his religious experience has ever worked.

Most people want to avoid this form of spiritual cleansing because it doesn't feel good. Yet something deep within us is saying, "Your old way isn't working anymore." This force within us is much closer to God, the Holy Spirit, and our true selves. This force within us wants to work for us. However, the majority of us would rather have comfort and certainty. Spiritual awareness and truth are rare goals for the ranks of the believers.

Yet, deep within us something wants to blot out the false light and move us closer to the light of truth. For most people, this appears to be darkness – perhaps even evil. It isn't. Instead, something deep within us wants to burn away the spiritual dross. Moreover, with such an essential cleansing, the eyes of the soul are cleared to pursue greater truths. In many of the Far Eastern cultures, the "dark night of the soul" is a badge of honor – an indication that this person is ready to move to a higher level.

However, in America the "dark night of the soul" is too often not seen as a badge of honor. The majority of Americans see the "dark night of the soul" as something to be numbed, overcome, exorcised, or "cured." At the point in which God is saying, "I want to move you forward," the religiously devout are praying that this liberation be exorcised. Valium, that little yellow pill, is used to numb this essential heretical crisis. Therapists are sought to free them from the healing that is welling up inside of them like a volcano. With the "dark night of the soul," God is stirring things up so that spiritual advancement becomes a priority.

A Call for an Escape from Beliefs

We are not trapped in some kind of original sin; only original stupid - ity. And stupidity can be overcome by a determined effort of intelli - gence.

— Ron Smothermon

Beliefs will not liberate us. They simply don't have the power to do that. All beliefs can do is weigh people down and make the spiritual quest more of a struggle than the dance that it was intended to be. Beliefs have no intrinsic way of leading people to the truth. Only personal experience can do that. Buddha did not tell his followers to believe in him. He urged people to work out their own salvation.

In Christianity, the issue is a bit more sticky. Salvation appears to be wedged deeply into the idea that one must believe in Jesus Christ in order to be saved. In addition, we have the apostle Paul claiming that belief in Jesus was/is essential for salvation. Having these ideas burned into our minds at a very young age can be quite powerful. No one wants to burn in hell. Therefore, the pursuit of belief becomes more a form of fire insurance instead of being part of a genuine spiritual experience.

The problem with such dogma is that it comes from "gospels" which were written at least a hundred years after the death of Jesus. They were highly edited to insure that they would fit into an already structured belief system. This belief system was also highly influenced by the Jewish belief system of which Jesus was a part. Rather than create spiritual liberation, these belief systems have contributed more to spiritual slavery than spiritual liberation. These rigid belief systems have created spiritual anguish for many, and spiritual certainty for those who want a pre-digested belief system. The end result is spiritual harm and a propensity to have spiritual experience blocked rather than nurtured.

Heresy helps people get free from stultifying beliefs. It allows people to use their God given freedom to search for a greater truth. It frees people from the idea that there must be one true religion and one spiritually correct set of beliefs. Heresy allows us to keep the power of choice alive. It helps us get beyond an ancient programming which was manipulative and inducing of slavery. In one of the greatest ironies, heresy allows us to break free of the conditioning of a false god and be free to search for and experience the God beyond this false god. To search for the true God, one rapidly comes to the conclusion that he must become a heretic.

Sadly, the majority of humans are stuck in their slave conditioning. They would rather be "certain" than free. The quest for certainty stifles the human spirit and chokes the human soul. Certainty and "being right" may feel good, but it rarely does any good. Certainty brings the spiritual quest to a dead stop and causes the mind to rest in sleep-driven comfort rather than pursuing a path more aligned with nurturing the human soul. The best antidote for all of this is an infusion of heresy.

Heresy: The Way to Personal and Spiritual Liberation

The seeker will discriminate between those things that tend to blur his vision and those which clarify it; such essentially will be his "moral - ity."

—Sri Aurobindo

Spiritual liberation is the goal of any human wanting to experience God. However, this spiritual liberation demands that the seeker move apart from "safe" and "certain" beliefs which have been weighing him down. The move beyond this stultifying belief-dominated certainty is a move toward heresy. Heresy is not meant to destroy religion as much as it is meant to nudge the human soul toward experiencing God in a more meaningful way.

Ironically, it is the Holy Spirit that leads one from paths that are blocking the experience of God. The Holy Spirit is not a destroyer, because that is not its nature. Instead, it nudges us deep at the soul level and urges us to gently put aside all of the false comfort of the past. This way, one can pursue a path with greater heart and greater possibilities of awakening.

Thus, this call for heresy is not about destruction or ridicule of what is past. Usually, the self-induced slavery of the past inspires a greater desire for genuine spiritual liberation. The heretic is not one who shouts in the streets. The heretic is instead a catalyst for spiritual growth. As he or she becomes more free, so are others able to move closer to spiritual liberation.

CHAPTER SEVEN

SUPPLEMENTAL NEWSLETTERS

PROMETHEAN FIRE

Statement of Purpose

Welcome to the first issue of *Promethean Fire*. We hope to be a trailblazer in an area where more than 99 out of a 100 people fear to tread. How interesting, how sad that as we advance technologically, psychologically, and socially, we still manage to deny painful realities.

In our ancient history lies an ugliness – a holocaust of the soul. Entities from another world, another dimension, another reality – the origin is not important – raped the free will of an emerging species and programmed that species to be slaves.

We are that species, paradoxically obsessed with freedom, yet programmed to be slaves. Whatever or whoever tampered with us long ago did its job well. Today, we walk the planet more able to talk about free will than embrace it.

Parents still see their children more as property rather than free souls placed in their care. Schools still eschew the love of learning and motivate with fear – and the promise of a higher place on the slave pecking order. Our work still languishes in a slave mentality with fulfillment and meaning lost in the competitive struggle.

Deep within our beings we have a slave chip – a programming which both allows slavery and promotes conformity to oppression. A ruling slave survives and prospers because the majority is comfortable with working longer hours at less pay so that a favored few can work fewer hours for much more money.

This began long ago. Researcher/author Zecharia Sitchin claims that the idea to create a slave race began more than 400,000 years ago. Others claim that it began less than 10,000 years ago. Finding out when it began is important, but nowhere near as important as recognizing that the human species is not a free species because other entities created them and programmed them to be slaves.

The Russian Mystic Gurdjieff once said, "We will never get out of prison until we realize that we indeed are in prison." Paraphrasing Gurdjieff, the four of us here at the Prometheus Project and Promethean Fire say, "We will not get free of being slaves until we realize that we were created to be slaves."

The high majority of people – more than 99% – claims that this is ridiculous. "God created us to be free," they righteously claim. The true God may have created us to be free; however, some entity, some force, someone genetically interfered with out natural progression for the purpose of creating slave labor. Unsatisfied with that atrocity, these entities also told us that they were God and that they – not the true God – should be worshipped. Whoever or whatever these entities were, we refer to them as the pretender gods.

We have no way of ranking the atrocity of this act. Rather than wallow in self-pity and rage, we prefer the bold path of self-awareness. As we grow in self-awareness, we can also grow in forgiveness. As part of that self-awareness, we recommend looking at what really happened thousands of years ago so that all of us can understand exactly what is happening now.

That is why this newsletter *Promethean Fire* exists. Join us in the journey.

Jack Barranger

Roland Masters Hus

Hiram Putney

Rico T. Scamassas

HOW WE MET

Through modem connected computers the four of us began dialoguing. The online world is an interesting cosmos. What began as one line questions and answers eventually emerged into an online forum. As we put our ideas to New Age, religious, scientific, and other forums, we sensed a kaleidoscope of views.

However, the four of us formed a bond. Each of us found in the other three kindred spirits and minds open to ideas which are both terrifying and liberating. We shared knowledge and learned from each other for little over a year. Then various other courageous souls urged us to print a newsletter. Many felt that despite the majority opinion, an aggressive yet compassionate minority was emerging. That bold minority nurtured the vision the four of us shared. They continue to do so.

THE TERM "PRETENDER GODS"

In an age with a plethora of terminology, do we really need yet another buzz word term? While we hope that "pretender gods" will never sink to the buzz word level, The Prometheus Project feels that an umbrella term is essential.

A group of "superior" entities did try to pass themselves off as God as early as 3000 years ago. They were pretenders because they were not who they said they were. They figured that because they "created" us that they had the right to pass themselves off as God. Because we didn't know any better then, we bought it.

So many terms and epithets abound. The Old Testament refers to them as the Elohim. Greek mythology simply refers to them as the Gods of Olympus. Sumerian mythology refers to these advanced beings as the Anunnaki. Classification becomes fuzzy when these sources attempt to sub-classify. In the Old Testament we have the Nefilim and the Raphiam – both subgroups of the Elohim. The Hindu religion has its own pantheon replete with subdivisions.

Thus, The Prometheus Project has its own term: the pretender gods. The pretender gods were a group of advanced beings capable of creating life, possessing immense occult powers, having greater technology and science which we presently do not have, and were capable of a devastatingly effective level of brainwashmg and programming.

They did not mean us well. Their main intention for creating us was to exploit us. While highly advanced in scientific areas, they were dreadfully retarded in spiritual areas. They were so atrophied in this area, that the evolving spirituality of their human creations became increasingly threatening to them.

The pretender gods so distorted our view of God that understanding the true God is nearly impossible.

They left about 2800 years ago . . . maybe.

IS GOD THE ENEMY?

To more than 99% of the people, this would be a blasphemous question. Even to the devout agnostic and atheist, God as non-existent or "long since gone" is a much more comfortable idea.

However, we at the Prometheus Project feel that the question is immensely valid. The pretender gods were the enemy. They warped our views of what a higher power was, what it could be. By claiming that they were God, they left a bad – and highly conditioned – taste in our collective unconsciousness mouths.

Theologian Paul Tillich came up with the concept "the God beyond God." We like that. It suggests that something lay beyond the highly perverted view of God which we received from the pretender gods.

Gnostic leader Stephan Hoeller, author of *Jung and the Lost Gospels,* states that a being higher than what we call God exists. What we call God is in reality what the Gnostic Christians call the Demiurge. According to the Gnostics this Demiurge was an insane God who "created" humanity, animals, and the world of matter.

While we at The Prometheus Project do not want to limit ourselves to pre-programmed beliefs, we do find the idea of a God beyond God fascinating.

AN INTERESTING CONCEPT

Antero Ali and Christopher Hyatt have come up with an interesting concept in their book *A Pregnant Shaman's Guide to the Universe.* They suggest that God should have to go through an application process just like any other hopeful executive.

Not just languishing in ribald suggestion, they actually provide the application. Making sure that people don't think that this is just an outrageous gesture, they conjecture how Jesus might have filled out the application.

This just might be an idea whose time has come.

RICO'S REVELATIONS
RICO'S ANTI-JEHOVAH BIBLE STUDY

Greetings, brothers and sisters. I hope you all have your Bibles with you. Today we're going to take the Bible study experience to new horizons. While most Bible studies happen in order to indoctrinate, our Bible studies have a different goal: We want to tell you the truth about your heritage.

Now I know that some are going to get real self-righteous and claim that we're into God-bashing.

Nope! Wrong! We're into Jehovah-bashing. The only gods that we want to bash are the pretender gods – high technology punks who thousands of years ago got so bored that they thought being worshipped would be real cool. If you sense that we feel that these pretender gods were a bunch of pretentious assholes, then congratulate yourselves on your perception.

Now would you open your Bibles to the book of Numbers, Chapter 21, and begin with verse 4.

> They set out from the Mount Hor by the road to the Sea of Reed to skirt the land of Edom. But the people grew restive on the journey, and the people spoke against God and against Moses, "Why did you make us leave Egypt to die in the wilderness. There is no bread and no water, and we have come to loathe this miserable food."

Now I think you can sense that the people are just a little bit agitated. I seen people at Jack in the Box bitch and moan because their French fries were soggy, so I'm going to editorialize just a tad and assert that these people had a legitimate beef (no pun intended).

But what does this compassionate, all powerful paragon of divinity do? Read on.

> The Lord sent seraph serpents among the people. They bit the people and many of the Israelites died.

This is what is known in Nefilim circles as Saurian motivation. If you don't understand "Saurian," this means that if people start to be a pain in the butt, you throw in a few snakes and the complaining stops forthwith.

Evidently, it worked.

> The people came to Moses and said, 'We sinned by speaking against the Lord and against you. Intercede with the Lord to take the serpents from us."

Brothers and sisters, despite our intense disgust, we do have to be fair. Ol' Jehovah did eventually take the snakes away. Life returned to a more predictable level of breadlessness and waterlessness. Yet, high up in his hovering craft, Ol' Jehovah wasn't hurting.

We need to ask ourselves a question. Why were all of these Israelites ambling around in the desert in the first place? Moses and Pharaoh had made their peace, so why did Moses and thousands of his people have to leave?

Once again, we need to open our Bibles and turn to the book of Exodus, Chapter Ten, Verse One.

> And the lord said to Moses, "Go to the Pharaoh: For I have hardened his heart, and the heart of his servants, that I might show my powers before."

What? Can we believe this! Two mere mortals work out a peace plan, and Jehovah mucks it up? Who does he think he is anyway? God? Now do a little critical thinking here. If this heart-hardening ego-trip hadn't happened, does this mean that all this desert rambling could have been avoided? No complaints; therefore, no tossing in of the snakes? Could it be that by working things out amongst themselves that Moses and Pharaoh were robbing Jehovah and his ilk of some wartime theater?

Who is this Jehovah anyway? If he's omnipotent, why does he have to show his powers? Is this good mental health for any divine entity?

Why would God want to harden anyone's heart?

Why would he want to bring on a battle when a peaceful means had been previously worked out? Yes, Cecil B. DeMille wouldn't have been able to give us that magnificent parting of the Red Sea in The Ten Commandments." But look at the other side: a lot of people who didn't have to die would have lived!!!

Aren't some of you brothers and sisters just a tad suspicious of this Jehovah character? Wouldn't you find a God who threw highly poisonous snakes among defenseless people just a little bit ungodly? Isn't all of this somewhat manipulative and psychotic? If not psychotic, would you at least consider "borderline psychotic"? How about highly neurotic?

Could the true "first cause" God be getting a bum rap because of such irresponsible antics? Can we really have proceeded for thousands of years without someone asking, "Isn't this just a bit uncharacteristic of a compassionate, loving God?"

I want you to close your Bibles now and pray on this. Ask your more conservatively oriented brothers how stuff like this never shows up in a sermon. I want the bravest of you to conduct rallies which give altar calls urging people to renounce the pretender gods. Just like good ol' Oliver Stone, we want you to stir things up. Jehovah was good at that. He put his nose in everything.

Thus endeth Rico's first ever Bible study for *Promethean Fire*. We hope you found it a blessing.

GREEK MYTH TELLS OF GOD MEDDLING

Thank you, Rico for that . . . ah . . . blessing. Lightning has avoided you once again. Now we move for a moment to what many unfortunately call our mythological past.

In Homer's *Iliad* yet another example of god meddling occurs. Two mortals, Paris and Menelaus, have a parley after nearly ten years of fighting the Trojan war. Paris stole Helen, and Menelaus wants her back. (She's really beautiful, so you can understand why the battle has gone on so long.)

Paris and Menelaus agree to stage a contest. The winner of the contest gets Helen, and everyone goes home. The contest wasn't even "to the death" – Just a good competition.

However, off on Olympus some gods began to panic. Nine and half years of good bloody battle was going to come to an end just because a couple of "mere mortals" got together and decided that they had a better way.

From their Olympian view the war theater had to go on: the gods just loved bloody wars. Thus, to insure that this little peace spasm would abort, one of the gods caused a spear to deflect and strike Menelaus. Because the mortals wouldn't dare suspect the foul play of the gods, they took the easy way and got pissed off at Paris and the Trojans. Thus, everyone resumed the bloody war and kept fighting until the gods got bored with it and let Odysseus and Agamemnon do their Trojan horse thing.

What gives me (Hiram) problems is that Homer was aware of this when he was writing his epic poem. He knew what the gods were up to. How come the tens of thousands of soldiers fighting for the entertainment of the gods didn't catch on?

A MINORITY VIEW ABOUT KRISHNA

I (Jack) am one of those rare people who has to suppress rage when I hear New Age and Far Eastern wannabees waxing "highly impressed" about Krishna. As for me, you can color me unimpressed. Having read the *Baghavad Gita* and parts of the *Mahabarata,* I find myself siding with Arjuna. He didn't want to fight because he couldn't see the sense in all the slaughter. He believed that peace could be worked out through dialogue. Krishna berated Arjuna severely and falsely suggested that spiritual values were related to waging war. Perhaps Krishna and his cronies were bored and needed yet another war as diversion for their highly boring stay on planet Earth. You have to remember that they didn't have television.

LETTERS TO THE EDITORS

The following "letters" came from on-line forums. We presented our ideas to various forums: new age, religious, spiritual, new-thought'scientific, anthropological, general, etc. At that time our log-on name was PROMFIRE. If some names seem strange, that's part of online experience. Each "letter" was answered by either Rico, Hiram, Roland, or Jack.

Dear Promfire:

Don't you think you're asking for trouble? People aren't ready for the idea that their teddy bear gods were really screwing them over.

Peabee

Dear Peabee:

We know that our premise is controversial. Truth has a funny way of frightening people. While our ideas certainly aren't mainstream, they are well researched by learned scholars, and these scholars have increasingly accurate material to support these ideas.

No one, including us, really wants to be right about this. We wish we were wrong. However, the more we discover about our past, the more ugliness we uncover. The great sadness is that few people are being made aware of these discoveries.

– Roland

Dear Promfire:

I had goose bumps as I read your stuff. Are you really going to put out a newsletter with stuff like this? If so, let me know. This is a revolution I want to be a part of.

Coyote Bill

Dear Coyote Bill:

You hit the nail on the head. This is a revolution, but we didn't start it. The idea that we need to get free of the gods so that we can experience the true God is an idea which rolled around before Christ. The Gnostic Christians were persecuted by the mainstream Christians because they believed that the god who created Earth and human life was insane. The idea of extraterrestrial beings influencing our early history was going strong at the end of the last century.

What is unique about the present time is that this appears to be an idea whose time has come.

At the beginning of the 1980's, a movie called *Hangar 18* brought forth the idea that ancient astronauts created us as a slave race. The film also suggested that they were coming back for us. Four years previous to that a feature film dealt with the idea of discovering technology left behind by ancient astronauts. Von Daniken's *Chariots of the Gods* film came out in the early 70's. Despite its propensity to "stretch mightily" in some areas, it has opened up some significant debate.

We're not going to be alone for long.

– Jack

Dear Promfire:

Are you people trying to start a religion?

Lilly

Dear Lilly

We have no intention of starting a religion. We think that the Prometheus myth is an archetype worth exploring. Something caused Prometheus to risk all and bring fire from Mt. Olympus to humanity.

Without requiring any belief system or structuring any sect, we want to open debate and especially provide an alternative view. The idea of the gods hoarding all the goods and tossing a few crumbs when they felt compassionate was – and still is – a counterproductive idea.

The gods are gone, Lilly, but their programming lingers on . . . and on . . . and on. Most of our brain lies unused and lies in darkness. The Prometheus Project wants to find ways to open those unexplored portions of the brain. That discovery may be the bringing of fire from Olympus to humanity.

The last thing we want to do is start a religion. That's what hurt us in the first place.

– Hiram

Dear Promfire:

Are you familiar with the RA material?

Lawrone

Dear Lawrone:

Sad to say that none of us are yet familiar with the RAmaterial. We have a bias against channeled material which we all are willing to admit might be closed minded.

Enough of you are asking us about the RA material that we think it's time that we take a look.

– Roland

Dear Rico:

I looked at the anti-God Bible study which you did. Of course, it is disgusting and immature. But then, I have found that I can never convince an immature person that they are immature. So why do I write?

I do ask you one question. Have you thought about what it would be like to stand before Jehovah in the final judgment?

June

Dear June:

Probably about the same as the poor slobs who had to endure Jehovah for 40 years in the desert.

– Rico

Dear Promfire:

Are you aware that a half hour program called "The Naked Truth" is being played late at night in Wisconsin and Michigan? This looks like one of those infomercials, but what they are selling is a group of tapes which state that religion is basically a conspiracy against the freedom of humanity.

If you are aware of this, we would like your opinion.

Joeknight

Dear Joeknight:

We are aware of the program called "The Naked Truth. " Two of us are very good friends with Jordan Maxwell, the man who is being interviewed on the tape. Five years ago, few people would bother to come to his religious conspiracy lectures. Now he is packing the halls. Jordan thinks we have reached a critical mass as far as religious dogma is concerned. He feels that most of it is going to collapse. We hope he's right.

– Jack

Dear Promfire:

All of you, aren't you tired of being like angry boys? Grow up and embrace the spiritual destiny which requires obedience and humility. You are doing great harm to impressionable souls.

Revkev

Dear Revkev:

Check that clerical collar: it might be choking you. We are growing up, and as we grow up, we are finding that bullshit, no matter how eloquently programmed, is still bullshit. People like you rammed God down my throat until I choked. You get these impressionable souls when they are really young, and I see that as the greatest harm.

– Rico

Dear Promfire:

Are you aware of how absurd your ideas are. Why are you even putting stuff like this on a scientific forum?

Doctorluke

Dear Doctorluke:

I assume you are a physician. I assume that you've heard of Ignatz Sempleweis who begged doctors to wash hands between operations. Instead of following such an "absurd" idea, those doctors operated on one patient and then went immediately to another — thus taking the germs of the previous patient.

The majority saw Sempleweis as absurd. Doctors first drove him out of Vienna, and then out of Budapest. I guess being "right" was more important than being effective with those doctors.

So it is with too many scientific types today. Carl Simonton cures cancer with visualization, but most doctors aren't interested. Zecharia Sitchin translates some Sumerian tablets and makes some "awesome" discoveries. Wake up, Doctorluke, the history of science proves that the majority has rarely been right. Read the material for yourself.

– Jack

Dear Promfire:

I am a high school sophomore who is a very devout Christian. I read your ideas on the forum last night and felt they were fantastic. I told my folks and they said you were doing the work of the devil. They said that the devil can make you feel very good about things which are evil. What do you think?

Bobby

Dear Bobby,

The last thing we want to do is drive a wedge between you and your parents. We know this about the real God: He wouldn't have given us a mind to think if He didn't want us to use it. I cannot imagine God becoming angry with any one person's search for truth.

Your parents care about you and want you to be a good person. That's why they are giving you warning. If they love and care about you, whether they are right or wrong really won't be that much of an issue.

Keep your heart open.

– Hiram

ARE WE STILL WORKING LIKE WE ARE SLAVES?
How Ancient Conditioning Affects the Way We Work: A Forum

Welcome to the first of what we intend to make a part of each issue of _PROMETHEAN FIRE:_ a forum where Jack Barranger, Roland Masters Hus, Hiram Putney, and Rico T. Scamassas state their thoughts about Promethean issues. Thanks to the technology of conference calling and a telephone answering machine which records all of this, we give you the first of our forums. Be aware, while all four agree in the PROMETHEAN PROJECT basic ideas, often they agree on little else. Roland is the moderator . . . of sorts.

ROLAND – Jack, your book _Knowing When to Quit_ has been out for about a while now. You claimed that people locked into a slave mentality would have a hard time leaving bad jobs.

JACK – I interviewed over 400 people for the book from 19 8 3 -19 8 7. I was shocked how many people remained in a bad job or bad relationship without thinking about getting out. I asked myself "What causes good people to stay in bad situations?"

RICO – Had you read any Sitchin _(The Twelfth Planet)_ by then?

JACK – No. I finally read Zecharia Sitchin's _The Stairway to Heaven_ one night after a cluster of frustrating interviews. About fifty pages in, Sitchin in his magnificent penchant for understatement says, "And fearing a rebellion in the mines the Anunnaki created a race of slaves to do their work in the mines, and humanity was what they created as that slave race."

HIRAM – That rattled you?

JACK – You better believe it. By that point I had interviewed about two hundred people, and I couldn't understand why they put up with so much and wouldn't at least try to find something better. Then I read this passage, and I'm stunned. I start thinking "Maybe this explains it."

ROLAND – Your book strongly hints that people are slaves without even using that word. You talk about workers being loyal to employers who don't have a shred of loyalty for them. You are the first person that I have seen who challenges *Winners Never Quit, and Quitters Never Win* mentality that is used by employers and spouses for manipulation.

HIRAM – Jack and I are both college teachers. We see the future leaders of America every day in class. Both of us are very frightened at the lack of vision and the compliance to mediocrity. While this has always been a problem in higher education, it's much more serious now. The students, for the most part, appear to be walking around in a trance.

RICO – They are in a trance. They're asleep. And they're going to choose work which allows them to remain comfortably locked in their slave mentality. Most of the young people I know are mental wimps. I don't think they have much of a future because of that lack of vision and competence.

JACK – I don't judge them as harshly as you do, Rico. Yes, they lack the vision and a sense of how to make their lives meaningful, but I don't see them as mental wimps. I see them more as people who are not yet aware of their acculturation and the devastating conditioning which keeps them from pursuing a nobler vision.

RICO – Like I said, they're mental wimps.

ROLAND – Douglas La Bier's *Modern Madness* shows how La Bier was given a grant to study the nature of work. Barely Into his seven year study, La Bier began to realize that work was a very sick process. His main thesis was "work is pathological." The company which funded him to the tune of more than $7,000,000 asked for their money back. La Bier said "You asked me to study work. I studied work, and these are my conclusions."

RICO –A real ass kicker that La Bier.

JACK – Unfortunately, both the hard cover and soft cover of the book didn't do well. People at this mid-point of the 1980's were not willing to face the nature of their work. I think this indicates that some heavy duty programming from the our ancient past remains intact. This programming helps people remain in jobs that they hate.

HIRAM – This actually begins in our educational structure. While my students are often lazy, they still can be motivated by the fear of a lower grade. Most will tell the professor what he or she wants to hear. Most will take the classes they are told to take despite the fact that many creative and acceptable alternatives exist within the same school program. They are slaves before they enter college and the high majority of them will be slaves when they graduate and move into their life's work. Eventually they will sacrifice their very dreams – and sometimes their souls – to get the right job and look good to other people.

JACK – Hiram, I'm not even sure that I can be as optimistic as you. I have seen those people when they go into their 30's and 40's. They are very, very comfortable with their slave roles. The only time that any of them become uncomfortable is when someone calls them on their slavery.

ROLAND – Like you did.

JACK – I didn't mean to. I just asked them simple questions like "If you're so unhappy, why don't you look for something else?" OR "Are you being fulfilled in what you're doing?" Some of them got angry.

RICO – If you do anything to challenge the slave conditioning of some people, they're gonna get pissed.

HIRAM – Work appears to be an extension of the slave chip. Most people work a nine to five job without even thinking about alternatives. Most people, despite having a majority in numbers, still submit to the will of the few in spite of accumulating evidence pointing out that participatory decision-making increases productivity. Most people do not see the real opportunities out there. They continue to believe their Olympian newscasters: Olympians Brokaw, Jennings, and Rather.

ROLAND – Do you think a time will come when education will embrace the challenge and priority of teaching students to look for good work opportunities instead of just teaching the three R's?

RICO – Hell, they're not even doing that.

JACK – Maybe that's our hope. As our educational system collapses – and it is collapsing very fast – we might see new ways to teach students. However, education will never really be effective until it begins teaching what really happened 4000 years ago and how that dreadful experience is affecting us today.

HIRAM – I tried getting some of the professors in the archaeology department to look at some of the archaeological discoveries which point to the reality that we had a very advanced race of beings here 3000 to 4000 years ago. They pull me off into a corner and tell me that I'm committing professional suicide by even bringing up such a topic in the faculty lounge.

ROLAND – They are terrified. They're affected by the same conditioning which was used to program humanity thousands of years ago. Don't rock the boat. Don't even talk about anything outside of the safe and secure paradigm.

RICO – Don't you dare de-condition yourself in any way, or we're gonna kick your safe and secure ass!

JACK – But there's nothing like going out and interviewing more than 400 salt of the Earth people who are terrified to do what they love to do, because some ancient conditioning says

"You must work and toil by the sweat of your brow, if you want your reward."

RICO – Good ol' Jehovah doing his Garden of Eden thing. We're playing that stupid tape over and over again. This tape has never worked for our spiritual benefit. Although it does keep us hoping that we'll earn the big lollipop in the sky.

JACK – You're so cynical, Rico. I'm gonna pray that your heart is cleansed of all that evil cynicism.

RICO – Cynicism is just a purer way of looking at the truth.

JACK – Sure it is.

ROLAND – The point is that we now have some very hard historical evidence from discoveries made during the last thirty years which lends much more credence to the theory that we were conditioned to be slaves in our ancient history. The *Atra Hasis, The Karsag Epics,* and newly discovered tablets of *The Epic of Gilgamesh* point out that these tales of "higher beings" aren't just mythology; these and other newly discovered writings are pointing out that this myth just might be history.

THE GODS OF EDEN – A Most Important Book

The Gods of Eden, ISBN 0-380-71807-3, $6.99, Avon Books.

Also available from The Book Tree, (800) 700-TREE or www.thebooktree.com.

One couldn't find a more controversially disturbing book than *The Gods of Eden.* Spending ten years researching war, author William Bramley came to the conclusion that UFO activity went up significantly during wars. That motivated Bramley to include writing about both war and UFOs. As Bramley probed deeper into both, he noticed a revealing consistency in his historical material.

Bramley began realizing that humans did not really want to fight wars. In fact, many resisted and were put to death in large numbers for refusing to fight. What

Bramley also realized is that thousands of myths tell of advanced beings who created these humans as slaves and coerced these slaves into fighting their wars for them.

What we in *Promethean Fire* refer to as the "pretender gods," Bramley calls "custodial gods," or the "custodians." They created us, they exploited us, and they were our custodians.

Bramley explores some interesting material in his research into the people who stood up to the custodial gods and attempted to help the newly created humans. Bramley calls these mavericks the Brotherhood. Sadly, even these mavericks who wanted to help became corrupted with power and ended up nearly as bad as the custodial gods.

This is revolutionary material, and it is very well researched. Most of the time it is a very exciting read. Sometimes, Bramley appears to be obsessed with getting in more of his research than he needs, and that bogs the book down a little. However, most of the book reads very well and offers mind-boggling insights into the early days of humanity and how we are being influenced by those events today.

Some of these revelations are both enlightening and upsetting. (1) The birth of Jesus was engineered by the Custodian Gods, but Jesus refused to go along with the plan and went his own way. (2) Zoroaster was one of the most revolutionary forces of the mavericks until the Angel Michael appeared to him and told him to focus more on obedience and get his followers to submit to his (Michael's) ideas. (3) Much of what is conveyed in the Old Testament is a horror story if people will only take the trouble to read the material for themselves. (One of Rico's examples in his Bible study was inspired from Bramley's research.)

What Bramley is horrifyingly making the reader aware of is that the gods of the past created wars as theater. Unfortunately, we don't appear to have gotten this nasty habit out of our system. Bramley mentions other areas in the Old Testament and other religious literature which points out that people who wouldn't fight for the Gods were slaughtered by those same gods who wouldn't tolerate having their theater messed with.

Buddhism and Taoism are the world religions most "untampered with" during the last four thousand years. Buddha was a genuine maverick who wanted to free men and women from the conditioned slavery of their past.

But Bramley feels strongly that these dark forces or "gods" are still with us. They insure that we go through incarnation after incarnation without remembering who we were in previous lives. From the spirit world, they keep humans in a robotic, obedient state focused more on serving than breaking free.

The Gods of Eden begins with an excellent chapter explaining the long painstaking work of anomaly researcher Charles Fort. Fort, after years of research came to the horrifying conclusion that we were someone else's property. Bramley has taken this idea one step further by suggesting that some force in another dimension has something to gain by keeping humanity enslaved and obedient.

With an excellent chapter on the founding of Mormonism, Bramley explains how new religions focusing on strict obedience are thrown into our history to ensure that we will remain subservient. While Bramley suggests that UFOs might be scouts for a physical force returning to claim their property, he wisely chooses not to develop that aspect. He has portrayed with great effectiveness a horror story which began thousands of years ago and continues today.

The Gods of Eden is a feast of legitimately explained conspiracy theories, exposing the potential of the Masons and other secret societies and showing the ugly underbelly of Judaism, Islam, Hinduism, and Christianity. The book is a feast of well researched argumentation for the fact that humanity has been enslaved for thousands of years.

For the truly brave, even among the spiritual explorers of the New Age Movement, we recommend you get *The Gods of Eden* and read it at a pace which will open your eyes without frying your paradigm. The journey will be both exciting and terrifying.

HOW TO GET INTELLIGENT PEOPLE TO ACT LIKE SLAVES
Slaving in the Mines in the Name of the Lord

For just a couple of minutes, assume that you are very high up in the ranks of the Pretender Gods. You have successfully held off all previous mutinies by promising your homesick mine laborers that you will create a work force which will do the dirty work for them.

The problem is that you are far from home. In fact, your home isn't even on the planet you are mining for valuable minerals. Thus, the only choice which you have is to take an animal that is relatively close to you as a species and do some genetic engineering. Because the miners want quick results, you hurry up the experiment. Behold, the first *Homo Sapiens*.

However, a few problems exist. In your rush to get out a slave worker, you goofed and made the first humans too intelligent. They quickly figure out how to make rockets, cleverly hide from work details, and eloquently protest. This group which was going to be labor-saving has turned out to be a real pain in the butt.

A hastily formed council drones on about how to handle this problem. New genetic experiments show a slight improvement, but basically this new slave worker gets bored easily, rebels against the idea of menial work, and prefers to commit suicide rather than toil in such a weary life.

After some efforts to "dumb down" this new species, you discover that they are too dumb to work effectively. They can't tell the difference between gold and lead. Thus, a higher level of intelligence must be retained with the next batch. Now how can these Nefilim keep the work force intelligent enough to work but still avoid all those riots, protests, and suicides?

The answer is to create a religion which promises rewards in the next life for sweating and toiling in this one. Convince these incorrigible humans that committing suicide in this life means that you will suffer forever and ever in the next. Convince them that they don't want to work because they were born bad, but if they straighten themselves out in this life by busting ass in the mines, they can goof off for eternity.

The all important motivator is guilt. Playing a cosmic version of "Good Cop/Bad Cop," you must convince these rebelling workers that you are the forces for good, despite all your exploitation. You must make them feel guilty for doubting any of this. However, they can work off their guilt by working in the mines, fighting a few wars, and worshipping you during break time. Any doubts and "Zap!," the mighty guilt-producing wrath descends. If you can convince these human workers that you are God and control everything, you can get them to do anything.

Of course, dying in any war is an automatic ticket to Paradise.

However, the bottom line is that once this religion is established, these newly created humans will work harder in the mines, give praise and worship to the hilt, and even work extra days . . . just to please their creators. We, the gods, will have to promise a few perks: fancy titles and an extra drink of water for the team which hauls the most blocks to the pyramid. Once you have drilled this into the humans, *they* will supply the pressure to their own. *They* will be the ones who will eventually become oppressive to their own species. *They* will now be the ones to assign the dirty work to offenders. (Actually, it's all dirty work, but the offenders will get the dirtiest work.)

Those humans who dissent will no longer need to be disciplined by you. Instead, the humans will remove even that heinous task from you. You will have to reward those who betray their own, but at least you finally have someone working your mines and worshipping you like you were God. This can be real fun.

The people who got to work least would be called Priests. All they had to do was continue the religious conditioning.

Our glorious psychologists and sociologists tell us that if we condition our subjects effectively, all of this could be self-perpetuating and could last for thousands of years.

What a system!

PLEIADIAN POOP
Aliens, Abductions, and Other Egregious Extraterrestrial Effluvia

CLINTON ABDUCTED!

On July 16, 1994, just at the point in which Schumacher-Levy 21 was crashing into Jupiter, Bill Clinton came back to the White House with a sheepish look on his face.

"Honey," Bill said to Hillary, "the strangest thing happened to me while I was flying back from Camp David. Right after we took off, there was this big, white light, and then I lost consciousness. I woke up and realized that I had four hours of missing time."

"You always seem to have four hours of missing time," Hillary said.

"My nose is bleeding, and for some reason, my butt really hurts."

"Bill, you promised that if you gave into the urge, it would only be with women."

"You don't understand, Hillary. I don't remember anything. I woke up with a sore butt and a nose bleed."

Clinton made some calls and decided to be regressed by alien abduction expert Budd Hopkins.

"Now we're going to go back to the moment where you saw the big light in the sky. What were you thinking right before that?"

"I was thinking that this woman was the best . . . Well, let's just say that I was lost in my thoughts. Okay, now I see the light. Wow! Now I'm awake inside this big ship. There are these really weird creatures about four feet tall with big black almond eyes and big heads. Now here's the weird part: they didn't have any mouths; I just heard what they were saying in my head. "

"What were they 'saying'?" Budd asked.

"They said I was trying too hard to keep up with the Joneses, and that I was spending too much time smelling the Flowers. I didn't get it."

"Anything else?"

"Something about leadership. I didn't get it."

THE ABDUCTION PRESS CONFERENCE

Once the press got word of the potential abduction, a press conference was demanded in the Rose Room of the White House.

"Mr. President, were you abducted by aliens?" Sam Donaldson asked.

"Well, Sam, what is it you mean when you say abducted? That word abducted has a mighty powerful spin. It's like the word 'infidelity.' You gotta be precise about terminology like that."

"Mr. President, were you abducted by aliens?"

"Sam, there you go again. When you say aliens, are you talking about; Iranians, Chinese, Kurds, Mexicans . . . When you say 'aliens,' that could mean a whole bunch of things."

"Did aliens from outer space take you into their ship against your will and humiliate you with a medical examination?"

"Sam, you know better than any reporter here that the President of the United States gets medical examinations more than any United States citizen. And you know that as Commander in Chief of the armed forces that I often will go on to a ship. So, yes, I have in the past year been taken onto a ship, and I have had at least one physical exam."

"But, Mr. President, did you actually go into space to have this exam?"

"Sam, my good friend Buckminster Fuller claimed that we are all hurtling through space on a large spaceship called Planet Earth."

"Mr. President. There have been rumors about your having frequent nose-bleeds, and that your butt is so sore that you haven't been able to sit down for the past four days. People who are abducted claim that implants are inserted up their nasal cavities and that various orifices are probed and often penetrated. Did the aliens do anything like this to you?"

"Sam, we have not established that anything out of the ordinary has happened to me. This is conjecture and projection on the part of a press that is obsessed with sensationalism."

"Mr. President, I think you're evading the question. We have heard you can't sit down. Was this because of the medical exam which had a rectal probe?"

"Sam, I'm going to level with you. Hillary and I were out on the White House tennis courts. I suggested some changes on the National Health Bill. Hillary got so angry that she told me I could take my tennis racket and ram it . . . Well, I think you get the point."

"Mr. President, you don't expect me to believe . . ."

"Hillary's a pretty strong woman, Sam. She took that racket and . . ."

"Mr. President. Surely you don't expect us to believe something like that."

"Sam, I didn't want to tell that story, but you forced it right out of me. I wanted to talk to you about the peace plan which some . . . entities . . . ah, people, kinda grey people, little punks . . . you know. Anyhow, they said if we don't get our act together . . ."

"Mr. President, are you talking about aliens?"

"Well, Sam. That really isn't the term I'd want to use. Hillary suggested that I use the term 'ultra-human quasi entities, biologically advanced beyond mundane human appearances.'In fact, Hillary said that if I used the word "alien," she'd take that tennis racket. and. . . "

RUMORS ABOUT CIA INFLUENCING *PLEAIDIAN POOP* ARE UNFOUNDED

The *plot in every corner*-conspiracy buffs are at it again. *Pleiadian Poop* has been lashed out against by a well known conspiracy expert as being a disinformation organ of the CIA. This is ridiculous, stupid, and really hurts our feelings. The CIAmade it very plain that the $15,000 they give us each month has absolutely no strings attached to it.

SAMJASE ACCEPTS JESUS AS HER PERSONAL SAVIOR

In a complete turnaround, Pleiadian spokesman Samjase has found the Lord. "This is absolutely wonderful," Samjase gushed." All that advanced Pleiadean philosophy couldn't touch some of the stuff Jesus has come up with. It's funny: I come here to save this planet, and I end up getting saved."

Samjase claimed that she made her decision at the June 1993 UFO Expo West when Norio Hayakawa began telling the audience how much difference Jesus had made in his life. "I was there incognito," Samjase said. "I know that we started all the Earth religions as a means to get you humans to work, but some of this Jesus stuff really touched me." Samjase is planning big revivals when she gets back to the Pleiades.

FAKE RAPTURE PLANNED BY DOG STAR PLANET

As if life weren't complicated enough on planet Earth, word is now spreading that the Sirians are about to launch a fake rapture. Born again Christians around the world are waiting with great anticipation to be lifted off this planet which they consider sin-bound and wretched. People other than born again Christians are waiting for born again Christians to be lifted off the planet, so that Earth will be a better place to live.

No matter. The Sirians – our intelligence reports confirm – are going to do a fake rapture, replete with blasting trumpets and lights in the sky.

When asked by *Pleiadian Poop* whether there was any truth to this, members of *Enki Saves* – a kind of evangelical, fundamentalist Dog Star sect, got very angry and said simply, "We were led to do this."

Pleiadian Poop reporters pushed hard for further information but basically ran afoul in any attempt to get more information. What struck some as strange was the cryptic comment made by Orgone, one of the *Enki Saves* leaders:

When you have a famine like we've had for the past 25 years, you get real hungry and find yourself saying, "Screw the prime directive."

PRODUCT REVIEW

The Pleiadian Potency Pill

After years of boring pictures of alien craft hovering over the Swiss countryside, the Pleiadians have finally come up with something worthwhile — something which will help the everyday Earth slob have a better life.

From the horn of the unusual Pleiadian Hippo-Rhino-Rangus comes an interplanetary aphrodisiac which the FDA can't touch. Now that's not to say that there aren't some side-effects. People, within minutes of taking the pill immediately go into loud obnoxious Tarzan yells followed by prolific bouts of braggadocio.

'Seeing a woman running around the room screaming 'I am the lay of the century!" seems to be a mass turn-off to about 98% percent of the men polled. The women polled claimed that this kind of behavior for men was typical.

Other problems lie in the fact that people are not following the directions on the bottle. The directions state specifically that no one should take this pill more than ten minutes before the sexual act. Increased reports of abused dogs and other animals point out that directions are not being followed to the letter.

Most women who take the pill want to be on top, and this plays havoc with men who think that the missionary position is the only decent way to fornicate.

Loud grunting and profuse evocations from different orifices indicate that perhaps the FDAshould indeed regulate this pill. The fact that most people taking the pill need three days to recharge is another inconvenient effect of the pill. However, most claim that they had wonderful dreams, and people who tried to wake them up found they had this broad smile on their face which lasted for the entire three days.

THE PLEIADIAN POOP E.T. QUIZ

Are You an Extraterrestrial?

Many people are discovering that they are not really from Earth – that instead they are an extraterrestrial soul in an Earth body. "How can I know?" many people ask. "Please, God, reveal to me that I'm something more than just some typical Earth soul" others plead. To help you know, answer YES or NO to the following questions and then score and rate yourself at the bottom.

1. At some point in your life as a child, did you find yourself eagerly awaiting adulthood? . . . . .YES NO

2. Do you find yourself attracted to the opposite sex? . . . . .YES NO

3. Did you find yourself bored at times during junior high school? . .YES NO

4. Do you experience mental pain when members of the opposite sex want nothing to do with you? . . . . .YES NO

5. Do you like ice cream? . . . . .YES NO

6. Have you ever said to yourself "Sometimes I feel like I don't belong here?" . . . . .YES NO

7. Does the fact that the Earth is going to shake, tidal waves are going to flood the planet, and hurricanes are going to ravage the planet give you a sense of absolute delight? . . . . .YES NO

8. Do you feel that most of the inhabitants of Planet Earth are a bunch of "useless eaters" who would deserve having their planet go through a pole shift? . . . . .YES NO

Scoring

If you answered YES to 7 or 8 questions, you not only are an extraterrestrial, but you are an extraterrestrial who's figured out that coming to Earth was probably the dumbest thing you've ever done. If you answered YES to 5 or 6 questions, you are definitely an extraterrestrial, but you haven't yet figured out how stupid your decision was to come here. If you answered YES to 3 or 4 questions, you are one of the Earthbound slobs that the rest of us are trying to save. If you answered YES to 1 or 2 questions, you are not only an Earthbound slob, but you are either two years old, or you are a member of one of those Stone Age tribes in the rain forest, or you simply need to get out of the house more often.

PLEIADIAN POOP PROSPERITY COURSE

With the imminent landing of the Space Brothers, lots of financial opportunities are going to unfold. With a pipeline to the Space Bothers, you will have an edge. However, with the knowledge of Pleiadian Prosperity Techniques, you will quickly learn skills which will put you far above the Earthling pack. Just a few of the many opportunities are listed below.

1. Learn the Pleiadian "Seven Sisters Chant" which brings gold and silver flowing into your life.

2. Learn the secrets of how to exploit other cultures and get very rich from it.

3. Make millions promising Earth people that they will be lifted off during the Earth changes.

4. Sell humans for labor in distant star colonies.

5. Make big bucks convincing people they have been abducted.

6. Get in on the ground floor of the ALIEN REPELLENTS market.

7. Secrets of the past life readers: the past lives which sell best.

8. "To Serve Mankind" recipe book – a hot selling item for aliens (and they pay in gold.)

9. Big bucks predicting Earth changes. (Share half of your profits, and the aliens will create them for you.)

Send in your name and address along with a $5.00 processing fee to Pleiadian Poop Power Prosperity Package, 1600 Pennsylvania Ave, Washington, D.C. 20500-0004. Note: We *really* think you should send for this!

THE JAKOV TAPES
Divine Channeling from the Id and Beyond

JAKOV'S DIVINE CHANNELING ABOUT THE SPACE BROTH-ERS

You may not be familiar with the trance channeling of the Russian mystic spirit guide Sergei Jakov – known in spiritual circles simply as Jakov. Jakov has had many illustrious lives in a human body. Jakov's channelings are fervently welcomed in the newsletter *Coyote Farts*. (Which has actually been "censored" from this book.) However, after much pleading and cajoling, Jakov has agreed to talk to *Pleiadian Poop* about UFOs and the Space Brothers. Because Jakov always speaks the truth and really thinks the "love and light crowd is a group of low level spiritual wimps," some might find Jakov's musings a little hard to take. Despite all that, we proudly present *Pleiadian Poop's* first ever channeling of Jakov. Tonight, Jakov will speak about the Space Brothers.

Greetings my brothers and sisters of the U. S. of A. I am Jakov. Tonight's subject is THE SPACE BROTHERS – those creatures who have been hovering around our planet. Before we get into this subject, I want you to know that everything that has been written in books about this subject is ca ca. Like in so many New Age pursuits, you have once again been duped by the Russians. Those low consciousness Slavic s.o.b.'s have perverted just about everything which smacks of New Age thought. Thus, I am here, my brothers, to separate the truth from the bogus.

It breaks my heart to tell you that the Space Brothers are not only immensely ineffective, but they also wouldn't know the truth if it bit them on the ass. In fact, if you listen enough to the same space commander long enough, you will realize these alien souls aren't very consistent. One month, California is going under the ocean; the next month it has been saved because of California's high spiritual vibrations. Stuff like this can make you very neurotic!

The most consistent thinking of these Space Brothers is that Earth people are all messed up. When it comes to superiority complexes, they are most consistent. However, this isn't much different than having a Californian feel superior when he's in Mobile, Alabama. However, this is the same mentality which causes the Space Brothers to think that they can help. To give you an example of how much they help, just about all of the people they have made personal contact with are crazier than they were before contact. Another area where the Space Brothers are highly consistent is in the area of showing off. I mean, even stopping in mid-air and making rapid right angle turns gets boring after a while. Flying at 10,000 miles an hour is impressive, but it simply isn't necessary for the hop from Chicago to Milwaukee. Okay, so they can fly circles around our military craft. To that I say "Big deal!" Remember when you were seniors in high school and wanted to impress the newly arrived ninth grade girls? If you understand that mentality, you are starting to understand the Space Brothers.

Another area which they have in common is that they think that your planet is going to shake mightily. They claim that these will be earth changes. The only changes which the earth needs now is getting the Space Brothers out of here. What should have been shaken was the confidence and credibility of all of those Space Brothers who promised that mighty Earthquakes that were due in '82. They still promised a pole shift before the year 2000, but didn't have any luck there either. However, that will do nothing to change the Space Brothers' followers who swear that we're going to have volcanoes hurricanes, earthquakes, and other goodies.

To show you how stupid these followers of the Space Brothers are, they claim that just before all of this happens, they are going to be lifted off and taken to safety. Don't any of these people read the Bible? How many were lifted off during that flood? Seven lousy people who got to build this crude submarine, and they were drunk out of their minds when they got back because Jehovah was still hanging around.

We have a proverb in Russia: " Halov Proviasky Belov Chantzchovich Pravda Lianov Shondrovaski." Loosely translated, this means "If you listen to lies in the face of the truth and do not boldly explore the evidence, you are not fit to shovel the droppings of a cow." I realize that if I offend you, you will not listen to what I have to say. Therefore, I'm being as gentle as possible.

Another area where the Space Brothers have an amazing consistency is the fact that they are really hot for earth women. It is a good thing that you men will eventually be needed to work in the future or you would have been history long ago. This is a bit of a weakness with the Space Brothers. Despite being told by their respective planets not to mess with earth women, they are a long way from home, and boys will be boys. Actually, some of the Space Sisters are fed up with this. However, they can not retaliate because they do not have the same attraction to Earth men. They think earth men are ugly as sin.

Now I will mention some of their gross inconsistencies. What bothers me is that none of these inconsistencies bothers you. For example, the group from Orion claims that Atlantis sank some 12,000 years ago. The mob from the Pleiades claims that it was 26,000 years ago. The group from the Dog Star claims that it was more than a million years ago. Anyhow, somebody's barking up the wrong tree. First, the bad news. No one can agree when Atlantis sunk. Now, the good news. All of the Space Brothers can agree that there was a continent named Atlantis and that it did indeed sink. That should be enough to create suspicion right there. But one thing about Earthlings: they really want to believe.

Now I'm curious if any of you who are absolutely orgasmic over the fact that the Space Brothers are here have had the courage to ask if those Space Brothers really have our best interests at heart. The good news is that they all have said that they do. When they take your women aboard spaceships against their will some women do end up feeling good about the experience. I am not sure whether this is a result of brainwashing or a commentary on the quality of lovemaking on Planet Earth. Those women who didn't enjoy it were able to be hypnotized into thinking that it was simply a physical examination. I guess if the Space Brothers are able to convince those who will listen to their intended altruism, they can convince anyone of anything.

Perhaps you consider me to be cynical about the Space Brothers. This is definitely not the case. It is like . . . oh, how do you say it in your baseball circles – I just call them as I see them. Perhaps I can help you further during the question and answer session. I will now entertain those questions.

QUESTION – Aren't the Space Brothers going to take some of us away when the Earth changes and the times of tribulation begin?

JAKOV – They do not yet realize that their etheric spaceships can not hold you.

QUESTION – Why?

JAKOV – Because they're stupid!

QUESTION – But can't creatures which have craft capable of speeds up to ten thousand miles an hour be worthy of being considered to be more evolved?

JAKOV – They are no more evolved than your missionaries who go to a town with no electricity and try to convince the natives of the value of their electric toothbrushes.

QUESTION – I'm 9 years old. I can't understand why the Space Brothers would be mainly interested in messing around with the girls on the planet.

JAKOV – In a couple of years you will have absolutely no problem understanding.

QUESTION – I just can't believe that the Space Brothers aren't more evolved. They say such beautiful things.

JAKOV – So does your advertising.

QUESTION – I don't in any way understand how you can make a comparison between advertisers on Planet Earth and our wonderful Brothers out in space.

JAKOV – Forgive me, I was wrong on that one. There is one main difference. While both do perpetuate lies, advertisers know that they are lying.

QUESTION – I heard that Benjamin Franklin was an extraterrestrial.

JAKOV – I'll bet you heard that one from the Space Brothers.

QUESTION – Who is responsible for the cattle mutilations?

JAKOV – Beats the hell out of me.

QUESTION – Hey, I thought you were some omniscient spirit guide.

JAKOV – Okay, if you want to play that game, The group from the Pleiades is slaughtering them for food for those abductees who can not adjust to a vegetarian diet. The Sirius gang is hunting them because they are the only animals dumb enough not to run away from the Sirians. The Venusian group slaughtered a bunch of them to help an Earthling writer get material for a UFO magazine. The Orion craft use cattle innards as backup fuel when their magnetic generators break down. The other 98% are accomplished by Earthling poachers who have found a fantastic cover-up.

I see that the channeler is getting tired, and my allergy to stupid questions is acting up again. Therefore, in the spirit of love and light I Jakov bid you good night.

FUWANGA SPEAKS
The Venerable Guru Fuwanga Speaks to the Masses

FUWANGA DESCENDS FROM THE MOUNTAIN TO ENLIGHTEN THE STUPID

Billy Bob Ananda was afraid that something had happened to Fuwanga, mainly because he was two days overdue for his monthly enlightenment session. However, after a month and three days, Fuwanga finally appeared at the foot of the mountain ready to enlighten the masses. Billy Bob acted as spokesman.

"Venerable Fuwanga," said Billy Bob, "we have seen many UFO sightings while you were gone. Actually, one of the UFOs landed, and three beings came out and said they wanted to talk to us."

"Did you talk to them?" Fuwanga asked.

"Yes,"

"That was mistake number one. The only way you're going to get rid of this riff-raff is to refuse to talk to them."

"Why? These are the Space Brothers. These are highly advanced beings who are going to save us from all the evil that is polluting this planet."

"And you believed that?"

"Yes."

"That was mistake number two."

"But, most venerable Fuwanga, these are technologically advanced beings. Their craft can glide across the skies at thousands of miles per hour. They can make a right angle turn without even slowing down. They can go in and out of solid form. I saw one of them fly right into a mountain. I'm out there screaming, "Watch out, you're going to crash into that mountain!!!" But the only thing which happened was that it went right through the mountain without making a sound."

"And that impressed you?" Fuwanga asked.

"That really impressed me."

"Guess what mistake number that was?"

"Come on, most venerable Fuwanga, these are exciting times! Don't you believe that these UFOs represent the reality that we are on the brink of a new age?"

"These UFOs are here for one reason," Fuwanga said. "They have traveled all over the universe looking for a species who would listen to their drivel. They were getting really desperate. Then they came upon this incredibly beautiful planet and started spouting out all this pretentious pap. To their surprise, people bowed down and worshipped these so called advance beings."

"And what planet was that, venerable Fuwanga?"

"Surely you jest," Fuwanga said, a hint of increasing desperation in his voice.

"Billy Bob, I want you to go back into full time meditation. I want to repeat this Zen koan over and over: "What is the sound of one brain resting?"

"Will that help me understand all the wonderful things which the Space Brothers are telling us?"

"Billy Bob, these same Space Brothers came thousands of years ago and laid all this spiritual crap on us. The only really great thing they did for us was to leave. Yet they left a group of people behind who have really screwed up the planet."

"And what exactly were these people, venerable Fuwanga?"

"Gurus. Christ, they're everywhere. People have this spiritual experience, and they decide they're going to become a guru. They get taken aboard a spaceship, and all of a sudden they have to start leading a spiritual movement. Someone tells them that they are really special because they've been taken on board. That makes about as much sense as going to a slaughterhouse and convincing all the cattle that they're special. At least the damn cattle who survived didn't go around telling all the other cattle that they were special. The last thing we need on this planet is another species of gurus."

"But, mighty Fuwanga, you are a guru."

"Yes, but there's a very good reason for that."

"Why?"

"I'm f****d up!"

"But, mighty Fuwanga, these wonderful Space Brothers have told us that they are here to help us advance and become more civilized."

"That's what you told the Indians a couple hundred years ago. Behold, I'm your Great White Brother. God has sent me to you to bring you to a higher level. Follow what we tell you, and you shall advance technologically and spiritually; and your lot shall improve mightily."

"Hey, that's exactly what the Space Brothers are saying," Billy Bob said, a smile breaking all over his face.

"Billy Bob we have an old proverb from the ancient Hindu writings: *"Parvu nasi oppt spermum extractus mit schmerzen y pollus langus oppt rectus stickum y so spiritas denken, sowie sollen cabeza oppt rectum sein."*

"My Hindi ain't too great. Could you help me with that one?"

"Well, because it is such a sacred writing, it loses a lot in the translation. However, loosely translated it states: "If a group of beings are sticking things up your nose and extracting sperm very painfully and then sticking this long thing up your ass, and then if you think that all of this is spiritual, perhaps your head should be where the long thing was."

"I don't get it."

"I think it's time for me to go back to the mountain. God, I can't believe how depressed I get after just a few minutes with this group."

"I'll bet if you talked to the Space Brothers, you'd feel a whole lot better."

"Billy Bob, how long have we been together?"

"Long time, Fuwanga."

"I love you, Billy Bob. I changed your surname to Ananda because I thought you were going to bring joy into my life. Oh well, we all screw up. Now listen to me. I'm going to give you a mantra by the great holy man, John Lear: 'If you see one of the spaceships coming, run like hell.'"

"But they said we're going to have this wonderful Golden Age. Of course, were going to have to have some earthquakes, hurricanes, tornadoes, floods, tidal waves, and volcanoes all over the place. Oh yeah, we're probably also going to have a pole shift which will wipe out half the planet. But other than that it's going to be wonderful. Hey, Fuwanga, you really look down. I've never seen you look so depressed."

Fuwanga didn't say anything for a full five minutes. Finally he lifted his head, tears rolling down his eyes and said, "It's karma. When I went to the other side, the first thing they told me was that I really screwed up and did the very thing that I had promised never to do."

"What was that?"

"Become a spiritual leader. They told me that I would have to come out at the worst time in America's history. I asked them when this was, and all they would say was, 'you'll know when they return. When they return, you'll be able to work off triple karma.' I never understood what they meant until you started talking about the Space Brothers."

"I'm having a hard time following you."

ABDUCTION TESTIMONY OF THE WEEK

We at *Pleiadian Poop* have always been jealous of the New Age la la's and the born again Christians who go to rallies and give testimonies. For those of you pagans who don't know what a testimony is, a person is giving a testimony when he or she stands up in front of a group of people and waxes lyrical about how their life has changed for the better since (1) finding Jesus, (2) taking EST, (3) doing T.M. meditation, (4) speaking in tongues, (5) joining Weight Watchers, etc. Left out of the equation is the poor slob who has been abducted by aliens. We decided to give these poor creatures a forum – a chance to give their testimonies. We will include the best.

"Hi, I'm Alan."

"Hi Alan."

"I'm an abductee."

"'Praise be."

"Before I became an abductee, my life was in a shambles. I couldn't pay my bills. The bank was about to foreclose on me, and creditors were calling up and threatening to garnish my wages. And I was only making minimum wage. Not only that, but my wife was threatening to leave me. She said . . . we, she hinted that my ah, you know . . . impotence. Well anyway, she just wasn't satisfied.

"We were driving home on this long, lonely road and we saw this light. Next thing I know, I was awake and very aroused. I mean we did it right there in the back seat . . . just like we used to do in high school. Ruthie said I was a tiger.

"But then I noticed that four hours of time were missing. I mean I was really good . . . but not that good. So we go to this hypnotist, and he regressed both of us.

You probably know what happened, and we're not going to bore you with all that. But despite all the pain and humiliation, some more good stuff came out of this. Hell, I would have been satisfied with just getting my potency back, but they stuck this thing way up my nose into my brain. Now I can get messages from them anytime.

"One of my creditors called up and said, 'This is it, we're going to garnish your wages.' Hell, I only make minimum wage, so that was no hoot. Then I hear this stuff in my head: 'Give him a bankruptcy number – any number – and tell him that if he continues the conversation that you're going to sue him for harassment.'"

"Damned if this guy did apologize and hang up."

"But that's not where the good advice stops. Another creditor called up and said that I had to pay off all of the debt now. That's when this stuff started coming into my brain again. This time I just spoke it as they pumped it to me:

"Listen, you insensitive lout, don't you know how to talk to people? I'll tell you how I'm going to work off the debt: I'm going to give a seminar on how you can talk to people – make them feel so good about themselves that they'll want to send you some money. It's all about self-esteem, you know. If you get people feeling good about themselves, you'll enjoy your job a lot more, and you won't be calling in sick as much. By the way, I'd appreciate it if you'd raise my limit to $10,000."

"They not only raised my limit, but they also hired me right on the spot. I make $200 an hour giving seminars on how to bring delinquent money in. All I have to do is send out a mental command, and black helicopters will be hovering above a creditor's house.

"My wife looks at me with a new respect. Life is good again, and all because of being abducted by those little greys. We're workin' out a deal where we're going to sell empty space on UFO lift-off craft once the earth changes start heating up. That one alone is probably gonna make me a couple million."

INTRUSIONS
"Into your illusion, I'll make my intrusion..."

STATEMENT OF PURPOSE

With this charter issue of *Intrusions,* we launch what will be a sane intrusion into the conditioned beliefs of The Holy Business. For thousands of years The Holy Business has strangled the collective soul of humanity. In the United States, our Constitution protects the right to preach misery and despair.

Laws freely protect cults that rape the minds and souls of the people they would indoctrinate. Religions continue to spread their slave doctrine with impunity. Televangelists pollute the airwaves with the dogma of five thousand year old entities who devastated the souls of their new creations. These five thousand year old entities brainwashed us into believing that they were the true gods, that serving them would lead to Paradise.

Yet, today people die for the right to keep these lies in the human consciousness. Wars are fought in the name of these soul-rapers. Thousands of years ago they conditioned newly formed humans to subvert their quest for freedom. Eventually, humans became slave labor for their creators – creators whom they thought were the true gods.

Into these lies we want to intrude. Our rallying cry is a line from song "Sometime to Return" by the group Soul Asylum: "Into your illusion, I'll make my intrusion." The four of us putting out this newsletter want to intrude and intrude boldly.

We want to intrude upon the highly conditioned slavery of those gods who lied in telling us that they were the true gods. We want to intrude upon the out of control rantings of the Pretender God priests who in the name of the true God continue the devastating conditioning initially begun thousands of years ago.

We want to intrude upon The Holy Business – that collection of beings who glean great sums of money to continue the conditioning that we are slaves and that we should remain slaves in the name of a god who departed long, long ago. We want to intrude on the belief mongers who insist that salvation is somehow gained by collecting the "correct" beliefs and go further into absurdity by claiming that those who have not collected the "correct" beliefs will suffer. We want to intrude on those belief mongers and perpetrators of The Holy Business: in their zeal they create hell on Earth. They scream loudly so that you will not hear the voice of the true God. They demand that you sing loudly those songs of conditioning which not only drown out the voice of the true God, but also continue the brainwashing of the pretender gods of antiquity.

We do not want to perpetrate evil. However, we do want to expose the five thousand year old con game which attempts to convince humanity that those who claimed to be God four thousand years ago were really God, they were not. Instead, they were pretenders. They were misguided beings who created humanity to serve their needs for a work force.

We have no desire to destroy people's faith in God. That has been accomplished already by the creators of The Holy Business and the pretenders to Godhood. They knew that if we found the true God, we would cease worshipping those who pretended to be God.

Their conditioning has worked well. For more than four thousand years we have embraced the conditioning of the pretender gods who demanded that we worship them, work for them, fight for them, and even die for them.

It is time to intrude on such insanity. Let us begin.

Jack Barranger, Roland Masters Hus, Hiram Putney, Rico T. Scamassas

UNIQUE BEGINNINGS
By Roland Masters Hus

Some of you might be aware that the four of us put out a newsletter called *Promethean Fire*. That newsletter's purpose is to focus on the historical basis and eventual fallout of extraterrestrial (or ultraterrestrial) beings who created us, enslaved us, and eventually demanded that we worship them as gods.

We coined the term pretender gods for these heinous creatures because they pretended to be gods when instead they were despicable beings who raped our free will and conditioned their human creations to work as slaves. Their conditioning was so effective that 5000 years later we still believe that this slavery is linked to holiness.

The four of us were excited because we felt that exposing the pretender gods was a holy mission – a way to break free of a badly conditioned view of God and move toward a more liberating view of God. We thought that our mission would simply entail helping people break free of bad conditioning. However, serendipity was to intrude on our path.

Driving down the Oregon Coast, Jack Barranger had planned to get in some quality time doing Zazen while sitting by the ocean. (Zazen is a form of Zen meditation in which the person empties his mind and focuses mainly on his breathing.) However, for the first time in Jack's four years with Zen meditation, he felt a strong voice speaking deep within him. Trained to block out all impressions, Jack tried to stifle the voice. However, unlike other times in Zen meditation, he found the voice getting stronger.

Eventually, Jack purchased two hundred 3 by 5 cards and wrote his impressions. Once written, he was free to continue with his meditation. What had originally intended to be a two to three day foray down the Oregon coast stretched to eight days. At the end of those eight days, Jack had more than 300 cards filled with what we now refer to as the "Intrusions."

Jack called us and told us what had happened. Being the arch-intellects that we were, we thought that Jack had surrendered to channeling or had been possessed by some discarnate spirit. However, after seeing some of the material, we realized that this was something deep within him tapping into what the theologian Paul Tillich referred to as the "God beyond God" – the true God who waits beyond our conditioning and Earthly illusion.

Jack's *Intrusions* – so called because they are intended to intrude upon the lies perpetrated by the pretender gods – touched something deep within us. Even arch-cynic Rico Scamassas claimed to be moved. Hiram Putney felt that once the lies of the pretender gods had been exposed, what was contained in the *Intrusions* would be the next logical step.

We all agree that all four of us are blessed in being part of a unique adventure. The time for well-programmed lies in the name of religion is over. The time for the excesses of *The Holy Business* is over. The time for slavery in the name of God is over. Now that the new millennium has begun, so also must end the slavery-in-the-name-of-God mentality.

This mentality has ensured that hell would continue on Earth. This slave conditioning – this four thousand year continuous loop tape of the pretender gods – has brought anguish and despair in the name of the true Creator who only wanted us to experience joy and liberation.

For a long time the voice of the "God beyond God" has been speaking, urging us to embrace the true nature of our souls; yet the blaring trumpets of the pretender gods continues through negative conditioning which most people have willingly continued through voluntary – and not so voluntary – brainwashing.

The *Intrusions* are meant to intrude upon what has kept us in spiritual slavery. A voice is breaking through. The intrusions which broke through Jack's meditation in December 1992 have created a space for intrusions in Rico, Hiram, and me. A movement is starting, and we want to share its essence with those who are ready.

WHAT THE INTRUSIONS AREN'T
By Hiram Putney

The *Intrusions* are not an attempt to start a religion. We have had enough of religions – the majority of which suggest that we should believe in a god who demands politically correct beliefs in order to enter paradise.

The *Intrusions* are not channeling – nor do they come from some discarnate being hanging around on another plane of being. The New Age penchant for *hang - ing out* with cosmic spooks delights us not. We feel that much of channeling is yet another attempt to manipulate humans to remain in slavery rather than pursuing spiritual liberation. The *Intrusions* are neither "the truth" nor "lies." They are meant to stimulate rather than manipulate. They are meant to open the eyes of those who are waking up to the fact that their eyes have remained closed for too long in piously restricted devotion. The *Intrusions* are meant to intrude on what has kept us in spiritual slavery. We hope that the *Intrusions* will contribute to your spiritual liberation.

GOD, RELIGION, AND HUMOR
By Rico T. Scammasas

Many readers of *Promethean Fire* have taken offense with what they refer to as scathing indictments of religion and religious people. Some have taken great offense from my Bible studies which use the Bible study format of conservative Christians and from that format "preach" invective and blasphemy. Others – sometimes including Jack, Hiram, and Roland – think that I come down too hard on those born again Christians who write pompous letters to *Promethean Fire* testifying that we have once again strayed from their well-conditioned view of the truth.

Jack, Hiram, and Roland don't restrict me because they believe that humor is a wonderful cure for pomposity. I suffered in my youth from Bible studies meant to indoctrinate me into the path of truth which guaranteed Paradise. I considered these atrocities – no matter how well meant – to be a disgusting form of brainwashing; thus, my use of the Bible study format was meant to be humorous and liberating.

Whatever Paul Tillich was referring to when he coined the phrase the "God beyond God," I know that that entity is laughing. He, She, or It is a force which desperately needs divine ass kickers and cosmic smart asses. More of the same voluntary brainwashing will only carve slavery tracks deeper into our highly conditioned minds.

I firmly believe that laughter is essential on the spiritual quest. If one stops laughing on the spiritual quest, one can be fairly sure that he has gone out on a New Age or religious limb replete with acceptance, hugs, and other forms of belonging which release endorphins, but fail to release the soul.

Genuine laughter terrifies New Age gurus and religious zealots. Yes, they claim to laugh, but it is the laughter of derision used to put down those who believe differently, or to provide a false comfort for those "wonderful" confessions of falling on one's ass while walking the spiritual path.

The force that intruded in Jack's life while driving down the Oregon coast – and daring to interfere with his sacrosanct Zazen – is a cosmic gooser. When allowed free reign, it grabs us by the balls and tickles us until we release our seriousness. Of course, many are going to insist that such a force is a pain in the ass to New Agers and conservative Christians alike.

New Agers and conservative Christians alike fail to understand that terminal seriousness was an invention of the pretender gods. Those pompous little shits had lost all capacity for laughter and projected their seriousness onto their very creations – the human race which was created to serve, work, and eventually worship.

When we dared to laugh – especially at some of their "divine" proclamations – they stomped on us hard. Jehovah, Krishna, Enlil – all found this laughter highly threatening because it launched us back into a state of the true divinity that is within all of us.

Thus, when I loudly released flatulatory gas in church, that was only mildly humorous. However, when Mrs. Hawthorne and Mrs. Gaynes turned their indignant eyes toward me in pretender god pomposity, the humor level quintupled because something divine within me knew that this was the only appropriate response to the sermon. Mrs. Hawthorne, Mrs. Gaynes, and all the other "true believers" preferred to sit quietly through their voluntary brainwashing without any flatulatory interruptions.

Jack's *Intrusions* are a wonderful breath of fresh air. They cry for a soul which is free and possessed with joy. Yes, they spoke of an ancient wisdom which is almost drowned out by the "joyous" chanting of "the saved." Yet they speak of a more pure divinity deep within us. Give Jack a ten for failing to follow the demands of his Zazen master and having the sense to write these things down.

Hiram feels very strongly led to write commentaries on these "Intrusions." I just pray to God – the real one – that he doesn't yield to terminal seriousness and erudition. I hope that he dances with the material. I love ye, Hiram, but for Christ's sake, lighten up!

As for me, I read the *Intrusions* and allow my perverse mind to hone in on the divinely absurd: a "Cheers and Jeers" right out of T.V. GUIDE making irreverent commentary on those punks like Jehovah and Krishna who pompously screwed us over. Intruding into my mind, just as steeped in holiness is Fuwanga, guru extraordinaire – the American Nasrudin.

Fuwanga is a holy smart ass, goosing people into divine awareness as he falls on his ass and belches forth platitudes of uproarious truth. Fuwanga was the Sunday school teacher I never had. Fuwanga is that cosmic smart ass who waits deep within our awareness, waiting to tell us a divinely off color story when terminal seriousness hath possessed us mightily.

Bear with me ye of conditioned faith. You might just laugh yourself into enlightenment.

INTRUSIONS WITH COMMENTARY
Bringing Light to a Unique Phenomenon

We wish to take nothing from Jack's experience of the "Intrusions." At his request, we have chosen to add insight and illumination to a significant event. Jack has no illusions that his material is scriptural and feels that his material is divine only to the point that it touches something divine within the person reading it. Roland Hus and Hiram Putney want to honor that humility and release any pretensions of rightness or certainty. In fact, we make commentary in the same manner in which Jack received the material – with a sense of wonder about the mysteries which lie waiting beneath our consciousness.

This is the very first *Intrusions* which Jack heard. It rattled him because it was not something which was in his realm of reality.

Wake me.
Wake me.

If you are bold enough to wake me,

you will wake something deep within you.

Do not project upon me your need for a Superman cosmic liberator.

I can liberate you to the degree that you will wake me from my darkness.

Pull me from the darkness of this ensnared sleep, and I will infuse you with a passion and a power for liberation.

This idea is not as radical as it might first appear. Nikos Katzantzakis in *The Saviors of God* mentioned that the true God is locked in sleep and needs humanity to liberate Him. The Christian Gnostics also believed that the world was ensnared by the crazy creator god (the Demiurge), who ruled because God had been forcibly locked in sleep. The Christian Gnostics also believed that the female goddess Sophia became fascinated and eventually entrapped in matter.

Bring light to the darkness.

Rouse me from my unwilling sleep.

Liberate your soul, and in so doing liberate me.

The sleep which comforts you so keeps me in darkness and pushes you deeper into the false light.

Understand that the false light

Keeps you locked in darkness.

The dark ones who created you needed you to believe that the false light was true so that liberation would not invade your thoughts.

Thus, you served neither darkness nor light.

You simply served the needs of another entity.

And instead of seeking liberation,

you sought approval.

Do not berate yourself for this.

For you were so programmed.

The dog who barks so fiercely at his liberators does not do so out of stupidity

. . . but instead out of conditioning.

Yet such actions do not serve you.

Free yourself from your conditioning.

Listen for the rumbling inside.

It is the song of freedom.

This speaks of dark ones who performed a perverse creation. While this is also an idea from Christian Gnosticism, it is not limited to this sect. The writings of the *Atra Hasis: The Babylonian Book of the Flood* speak of creators who made the human race as a slave race to do their menial work. This is also mentioned in the *Kharsag Epics* and *The Epic of Gilgamesh*. The Mayan scriptures – the *Popol Vuh* – suggest six different creations until the gods could create a human who would praise the pretender gods and still do hard work with question. Throughout what so many insist on calling "mythology," the tales of the dark gods who programmed us vividly come forth.

What you call the light keeps you in darkness.
What you call liberation keeps you enslaved.
Instead of a passion for freedom,
you seek instead for chains,
and the chains give you false comfort.

You cry, "I have found the light,"
and you march deeper into darkness.
The one who will free you makes no demands.

The one who will free you does not insist on beliefs.

The one who will free you needs you to free him.

Cease your watching of the sky and look within for
a liberator waiting to be liberated.

Once again we have the paradox of the liberator needing to be liberated. What is being addressed here is an essential synergy – the joining with a force which lies beyond conditioning and religion. What also is addressed here is what also shows up in many of the *Intrusions*: a warning to see false light for what it is. During the 1980's and up to the present, many spiritual works have warned of a false light. Kyle Griffith in *War in Heaven* warned people to avoid the light as one made the transition from this life into the next. Whitley Strieber in *Communion* and William Bramley in *The Gods of Eden* also addressed the idea of the "trick of the light" – that false light seen when one moves from this awareness to the next level in death. Admittedly, this is far from being a popular idea; however, the idea that the light seen after death is a Godly light is still an untested idea. *The Tibetan Book of the Dead* and *The Egyptian Book of the Dead* also warn of false "lights" in the realm of the dead.

Also addressed here is the potential reality that the light of religion is a false light which only leads to darkness. This idea isn't new; it was embraced strongly in the middle of the 19th Century and had continued into the 21st Century.

You do not fully understand power and empowerment.

If you need to be comfortable in your quest,
You will limit your choices.

If you need the comfort of working with a group of people,
Your quest will be blunted. Transcend your world view.
Transcend the world view of others.

You came here to please no one.
You came to empower people.

If you need your empowerment to come from ideas which are aligned with your beliefs,
you ask the one empowering you to block your empowerment.

First, a bit of etymology. The word "comfort" is a bastardized word in the English language. Coming from two Latin words – "cum" and "forte" – the word comfort originally meant empowerment. Thus, when Jesus claimed that he would send a comforter, he was not talking about a great dispenser of Valium. Jesus was instead talking about a force that would empower people.

Even the most conservative bastions of Christianity talk about a Trinity; however, the Holy Spirit is too often relegated more to the realm of talk than experience. It is basically ignored (except when professed in dogma or doctrine). None of the four of us – Rico included – has any problem with the idea that a force known as the Holy Spirit can empower people.

The dark gods made up sin
to manipulate you with guilt.

The true God does not see sinners,
but instead sees people of wonder
who judge themselves harshly.

The dark gods are gone.
No more gain comes from
judging yourselves harshly.

Give it up, and dance once again.

The Greek word for sin is "hamartia." In the study of Greek literature, this meant a tragic flaw. However, the Biblical Greek meaning was more compassionate and suggested an act of falling short of the target. No grief or judgment was intended. Many used it as a metaphor, suggesting an archer shooting at a target and having his arrows fall short. Within this metaphor was the acknowledgment that someone was making an effort – and was moving toward the target. This might explain why Jesus was more comfortable with prostitutes and tax collectors. Unlike many religious people of his day, they were at least doing something.

INTRUSIONS WITHOUT COMMENTARY

While the *Intrusions* have been both collected and numbered, we choose to present a representative sampling of them. Eventually, we will publish all of them in a book. However, for now, the only way to read these *Intrusions* is through this newsletter. The name *Intrusions* suggests an invasion – an actual intrusion upon the spiritual consensus reality. We want to intrude because we firmly believe that the spiritual consensus reality has lost its soul.

Deep within you is a voice – the voice of the God beyond God. This voice will not lead you to sing hymns of repression or urge you to chant the poetry of self-denial.

What created you at the level of the soul will never ask you to negate yourself at any level.

This voice is the voice of your liberation – your walk away from conditioned responses etched deep in your consciousness thousands of years ago.

Be still and listen for this deep voice.

Decondition yourself.

If you have a choice between reading a spiritual book and frolicking in the ocean, by all means frolic in the ocean.

If you have a choice between hearing a New Age speaker and participating in a pillow fight, please choose the pillow fight.

If you have a choice between going to church and swinging on a swing, opt for the swing.

If you are worried about being too heavy for the swing, be more concerned about how heavy most church services make your soul.

How will you know when you have found the right church? When you break into laughter ten minutes into the service and continue laughing long after the benediction.

You shall know the truth, and the truth will set YOU free, but first it's going to frighten you.

You shall know the truth, and the truth shall set you free, but first it's going to make you angry.

So many say, "I have found the truth," when all they have experienced is a rush of endorphins to their brain.

As soon as a person claims, "I understand the truth," he no longer has the truth.

You ride happily on the merry-go-round figuring that if you can catch the brass ring, then you will truly be happy.

Wake up, slave-obsessed beings, it is not the brass ring which you want.

What you really want is to get off the merry-go-round.

Wake up, those of you who want to be free.

You have judged your freedom by the quality of your chains.

Those of you who have copper chains feel superior to those whose chains are made of lead.

However, those of you who have copper chains do not yearn for freedom as much as you do for a higher quality of chains to restrict you.

"Oh, if only I could switch from copper chains to gold chains," you say. "Let me have gold chains and then I will truly be happy again."

Do you not understand? This is not freedom, but only a higher quality of chains.

Your mission in life is to get free of the chains.

Then you can begin leading others to freedom.

The pretender gods demanded obedience.

The true God – the God beyond God – wants all sentient beings free.

Subservience is of the pretender gods.

Liberation is of the God that is beyond God. When you bow to the manipulative pretender gods, you negate yourselves.

To find the God beyond God, you must liberate yourselves.

Negating yourselves keeps the true God locked in sleep.

Embracing your true selves empowers the true God.

When the true God is empowered, freedom comes.

You walk in darkness because you cannot learn from myth. You convince yourself that ancient peoples made up stories using their highly inventive imaginations.

How long will you continue with this highly deceptive denial?

By doing this you deny your history . . . and your heritage. By surrendering to such an inane theory, you deny what you must face in order to secure your liberation.

You have remained slaves for too long.

Wake up!

If you continue this folly, two thousand years from now highly intellectual but badly misinformed teachers will tell their students that there really wasn't an atom bomb explosion at Hiroshima. No, they will say, this is just a symbolic explosion of awareness in a symbolic war between good and evil.

And this disease AIDS which killed millions of people. Those erudite explainers of myth will tell their students that this wasn't an actual disease but instead simply a metaphor for spiritual death, something which the people of the 20th and 21st centuries made up in their heads to point out a spiritual truth.

And these things which we call flowers. Highly "intelligent" teachers in the 40th century will tell their students that their really weren't any such thing as flowers. This was just mythological wishful thinking.

These, so said the interpreters of myth, were created in the human mind to compensate for a lack of aesthetic beauty.

How brilliant is the human mind. So brilliant that it can make the stupid appear intelligent. And so have we done when we dare to think that myth was the invention of overactive minds.

This invention was not done by the tellers of the myths. They were merely reporting their history. The invention was done instead by the interpreters who followed later, and the price of this wrong interpretation is the rape of your very souls.

Look to your past history and find the truth. While it will first be upsetting, it will eventually liberate you.

I tell you of a time on planet Earth, a time when men were locked in slavery because cruel beings created a race of humans to be slaves.

To insure that these slaves would work without rancor or revolt, the slavemasters lied and told the slaves, "Because we created you, we are your God."

And the slaves believed because they did not yet possess the mental skills to realize that their slave masters were only pretending to be gods. Thus, when the false gods said, "We are truly gods," the slaves believed.

This believing has gone on for too long. Cease your conditioned beliefs that you might leap free.

You do not realize how much of your life is determined by your need for approval. If you could get free of this binding need for approval, you would accomplish feats beyond your dreams.

However, it is difficult for one who has been conditioned to serve and do menial work to think of himself accomplishing God-like feats.

One who has been programmed to serve, continues his toil of dreams of reward in the future. Once one has thrown off the shackles of his conditioning, he seeks out the passions of his heart and begins experiencing high creativity and great rewards in the present.

Beware of people who tell you that they are free. Free people do not have to inform you of their freedom.

WHAT HAPPENED ON THE OREGON COAST:
From the Horse's Mouth
Jack Barranger

The genesis of the *Intrusions* was for me a powerful event. I had left my Portland friends Bill and Julie after a four day Christmas visit. My plan was to relive a 1976 journey down the Oregon coast and this time spend two to three hours a day doing Zazen – a discipline I learned as part of a writing assignment about Zen Meditation many years ago.

My first day's drive was a dreary, rainy experience which left me at the top of Oregon's coast in the town of Seaside. My uppermost memory of that evening was going for a walk after the rain stopped and having the temperature quickly drop fifteen degrees just at the point where I was two miles from my motel.

The next day was sunny, and I began my Zazen in earnest. My plan was to find a quiet beach for 30 to 40 minute periods of Zazen and Kinen (deliberate walking with no thoughts). My first forty minute venture was successful: I could feel the strain of the previous semester's teaching beginning to unravel.

I drove another fifteen miles and found another gorgeous beach spot with no people. Fifteen minutes into this session, I sensed something deep within me was speaking. Those trained in Zen meditation know that thoughts are to be acknowledged and then ignored. Being the good little Zen boy, I attempted to let the thoughts pass.

However, unlike a plethora of unrelated thoughts, these thoughts had an order and a repetition. This was not like Helen Schuchman's command that "This *is A Course in Miracles;* please take notes." Instead, this was a very deep feeling which demanded to be expressed in words.

I had had experiences like this in Denmark. Czechoslovakia, Texas, and California. The experience was not strange to me, but this time it had a much stronger clarity and urgency. I know that whatever was speaking deep within me was not going to let up until I had written the material down.

I had with me about forty 3 by 5 lined note cards. I went to the car, got the cards, and wrote down words representing the feelings deep from within. I was strongly aware that this was not something I was making up. I was sure of this when I would be driving and another "intrusion" would announce itself.

Whatever generated these *Intrusions* had no aesthetic sense of beauty – no appreciation for the fact that I would prefer to be inspired while I was driving along some magnificent stretch of road with a beautiful view. Not so. These wonderful *Intrusions* plagued me while eating seafood dinners, registering for a motel room, or even in the midst of passing a slower car.

As I wrote down over two hundred of these pithy revelations, I sensed that this was something which was blossoming at a perfect time for me and American society. I knew that I could not make these statements up in my waking mode of consciousness; yet I still felt that these statements were coming from something which is unique to me.

One aspect which helped me realize they weren't something which I was making up was the fact that I didn't believe some of the statements I was writing. Put another way, some of the statements I was writing didn't appear to be a part of my paradigm. The idea of God asking to be rescued from sleep struck me as strange; I felt that the true God would be the cosmic awakener who didn't need any help from humanity.

Yet, what I was getting from these *Intrusions* was a God force claiming that the process of waking up from our sleep of illusion was a dual act. This God force was saying, "You help me wake up; I'll help you wake up."

I wrote these *Intrusions* down because they smacked of that greater truth which Rico, Hiram, Roland, and I had been nipping at in our newsletter, *Promethean Fire*. They felt both right and revolutionary.

As I was writing these *Intrusions* down, I had a sensed that I was not the only receiver of what was being broadcast. I sense that a cosmic wake up call was being generated from the soul level of many people. The excesses of religion and the growing excesses of the New Age Movement lean more toward ego-gratification and ego-terror than soul liberation.

A force – perhaps at the cellular level, preprogrammed to unleash a wake up call – had decided to rudely intrude upon slavery in the name of free will. This force is compassionately, yet with increasing firmness, saying, "Enough."

What happened on the Oregon coast was not a highly evolved source selecting a special person for a new religion. What happened on the Oregon coast was prob-ably one of many divine heretics remaining open to voices which will help him restore sanity to the spiritual quest. The time for a genuine spiritual renewal is ripe

---

WERE YOU MEANT TO BE AN INTRUDER?
The Real Cosmic Mission
Jack Barranger

We live in interesting times. With crime passing the point of critical mass, we focus more on anything which resembles a safety net – even if it is sterile and bor-ing. As political promises fade to unquestionable reality, we look beyond the phys-ical realm for realities both etheric and dependable.

However, we are starting to realize one brutal reality: if stability means more of the same, the prospect is as unbearable as any apocalyptic scenario.

Born as an alternative to materialist prosperity and traditionalist religion, the New Age movement stepped up in earnest in the mid-sixties and blossomed in the seventies. By the 1980's this movement had been co-opted by the "me generation" and lost its cutting edge despite making millions for self-appointed purveyors of truth. By the 1990's the New Age movement was a beached whale hawking spiri-tual hot dogs – its force swamped in channeling, crystals, Christs-in-training, and anything which would generate a buck.

Despite the sins of Televangelists and new entries to the religion-of-the-week, religion flourished for the most part and continued to stifle souls yearning for lib-eration. In tandem with New Age channeling, the 5,000 year old concept of sur-render was gold-plated to the point where giving up in the name of God was testi-fied to as being the ultimate spiritual release.

As an added "thrill," the prospect of a benign invasion by the Space Brothers invaded a higher percentage of people seeking for a way out. Interestingly enough, they are referred to as *intruders*, and the people taken against their will are referred to as contactees.

At a conference in Berkeley, I listened as five Ph.D's attempted to brainwash their audience of 550 into believing that all of this was "something wonderful" and we should stop resisting this cosmic intrusion. All five insisted that "abductees" was too negative a term and these abductees would henceforth be known as "expe-riencers."

All of this indicates that some kind of cosmic con job has been going on for a very long time. The "experiencers" are still put through – according to them – very painful medical examinations and still experience consistently interrupted sleep and deep levels of depression.

In the name of religion, people still find joy in testifying to what horses asses they are without the Lord. Despite increasing evidence from history and anthropology, most people think it's fine that Jehovah killed his own Israelites by throwing poisonous snakes in their midst and demanded that peace-loving Israelites slaughter peace-loving Cannanites. A mental surrendering of reasoning resolves this by claiming that God in His wisdom knows what He's doing; who are we to question?

This insanity has gone on for hundreds of years with little or no intrusion. The last historical intrusion were the German and Czechoslovakian reformations of the Renaissance. While centered around shaky theology, they still respected a human's right to experience more freedom in his or her relationship to God.

A deeper Reformation is needed – this time by people bold enough to claim that Jehovah, Krishna, Enki, Enlil, Isis, and Osiris were not gods. In America we remain stuck in a Jehovah complex which eschews freedom and embraces slavery in the name of God.

Into all of this lunacy an intrusion is highly appropriate. In fact, an intrusion is essential. The programming of the past has continued long after Krishna, Jehovah, Enki, and their ilk got bored and left. What they left behind was a badly programmed species which somehow links holiness with continuing their conditioning to remain slaves.

Thankfully, intruders have come and infused the collective consciousness with the possibility of breaking the bonds of pretender god conditioning and liberating the soul from its comfortable addiction to slavery: Buddha, Jesus, Lao Tse, Mohammed.

However, the age of the individual liberator may have passed. Souls eager to help may have come into bodies for the mere purpose of stirring things up – intruding into the false comfort generated by channeled ideas, religious dogma, and consensus reality. This time a high number of souls may have come into this three dimensional reality to shine some light into the dark corners where false light comforts, but fails to illumine.

If you feel like you might be one of those divine intruders, for once don't laugh it off. Stay apart from your conditioned ideas awhile and consider that the God beyond God might have sent out a force and that you might be one of them.

FUWANGA SPEAKS
The Venerable Guru Fuwanga Speaks to the Masses
Rico T. Scamassas

FUWANGA DESCENDS FROM THE MOUNTAIN TO ENLIGHTEN THE STUPID

For too long has Fuwanga been gone. Fuwanga claims that he needed meditation time. However, the born again Christians claimed they drove him out with a combination of prayer and prolonged hymn singing. Not to be outdone, the El Cajon High Consciousness Center – meeting place of the New Age cognoscenti – claimed they paid Fuwanga to disappear because he was making it hot for highly prosperous New Age leaders.

Despite all of this Fuwanga appeared once again.

Super-quester Billy Bob Ananda asked the first question.

"Venerable Fuwanga, what is the meaning of karma?"

"Karma is highly overstated," Fuwanga said. "People claim something happened to them because they had bad karma. Horse ca ca! People have bad things happen to them because they are stupid. Karma is yet another ecclesiastical cover-up for stupidity. Show me someone who claims they have bad karma, and I'll show you a stupid person."

"But karma has got to have some spiritual meaning."

"Yes," Fuwanga sighed, "karma does have some spiritual validity. The great powers of the Paradise Brotherhood claim that they have been practicing godliness for thousands of years now and they can let just about every sin go. However, there's one group of people who really have the Paradise Brotherhood pissed off because they just don't seem to get it. So they have lots of karma."

"And what group would that be, venerable Fuwanga?"

"Spiritual leaders. They are told over and over again. If you go out and do that spiritual leadership again, it's your ass. But they just don't learn. It's like a disease. Right before they come out into a body, they swear, 'So help me I promise I won't get seduced into being a spiritual leader.' Then they get into the earth plane, start saying those masses and sing those hymns, and they just get sucked right in."

"But, venerable Fuwanga, there is something slightly amiss here. Aren't you a spiritual leader?"

"I have to confess that I am."

Then why don't you stop it if it means all this bad karma?"

"God knows, I've tried to quit. This time I thought I was really going to make it. For fifteen years I sold real estate. I said this time I'm going to make it through a whole lifetime without becoming a spiritual leader. I was doing fine until I heard Handel's *Messiah*. The ol'juices started flowing again – kinda like a spiritual nicotine fit. I just had to give spiritual guidance."

"Was it the sense that you were really helping people?"

"Basically it was the women and the money."

"I don't understand."

"You start doing those pastoral counseling sessions and these sensuous women are adoring you, panting heavily, pulling out their checkbooks, and something deep inside of you says, Why work for a living?'"

"Do you think you will be forgiven?"

"Not a chance. I've done this four lifetimes in a row. Last time they made me stand watch as people came over from their earth lives. I watched as clarity finally returned and they realized that Paradise was out."

"That must be horrible!" Billy Bob said.

"Hell no!" Fuwanga said. "That means you have to spend an extra long time in Paradise. It's misery. You sing hymns fourteen hours a day. We start at the beginning of the hymn-book and go right to the end. Incorrigible offenders gotta sing 'The Old Rugged Cross'fifty times in a row. All five verses. Some people after thirty verses fall down on their knees and scream, "Lord, I'll never do it again!"

"Does the name Fuwanga have any spiritual meaning?"

"It's Sanskrit – a very old language. However, the name is very difficult to translate."

"Could you give us an idea?"

"Loosely translated, it means Horse's Ass Guru Trouble Maker."

INDEX

101

Past Shock: The Origin of Religion and Its Impact on the Human Soul, by Jack Barranger.  Twenty years ago, Alvin Toffler coined the term "future shock" — a syndrome in which people are overwhelmed by the future. *Past Shock* suggests that events that happened thousands of years ago very strongly impact humanity today. Technologically advanced beings created us as a slave race and in the process spiritually raped us. This book reveals the real reasons why religion was created, what organized religion won't tell you, the reality of the "slave chip" programming we all have to deal with, why we had to be created over and over again, what really happened in the Garden of Eden, what the Tower of Babel was and the reason why we were stopped from building it, how we were conditioned to remain spiritually ignorant, and much more. Jack exposes what he calls the "pretender gods," advanced beings who were not divine, but had advanced knowledge of scientific principles which included genetic engineering. Our advanced science of today has unraveled their secrets, and people like Barranger have the knowledge and courage to expose exactly how we were manipulated. Learn about our past conditioning, and how to overcome the "slave chip" mentality to begin living life as it was meant to be, as a spiritually fulfilled being. **ISBN 1-885395-08-6 • 126 pages • 6 x 9 • trade paper • illustrated • $12.95**

Of Heaven and Earth: Essays Presented at the First Sitchin Studies Day, edited by Zecharia Sitchin. Zecharia Sitchin's previous books have sold millions around the world. This book, first published in 1996, contains further information on his incredible theories about the origins of mankind and the intervention by intelligences beyond the Earth. Sitchin, in previous works, offers the most scholarly and convincing approach to the ancient astronaut theory you will most certainly ever find. This book offers the complete transcript of the first Sitchin Studies Day, held in Denver, Colorado on Oct. 6, 1996. Zecharia Sitchin's keynote address opens the book, followed by six other prominent speakers whose work has been influenced by Sitchin. The other contributors to the book include two university professors, a clergyman, a UFO expert, a philosopher, and a novelist—who joined Zecharia Sitchin in Denver, Colorado, to describe how his findings and conclusions have affected what they teach and preach. They all seem to agree that the myths of ancient peoples were actual events as opposed to being figments of imaginations. Another point of agreement is in Sitchin's work being the early part of a new paradigm—one that is already beginning to shake the very foundations of religion, archaeology and our society in general. **ISBN 1-885395-17-5 • 164 pages • 5 1/2 x 8 1/2 • trade paper • illustrated • $14.95**

Space Travelers and the Genesis of the Human Form: Evidence of Intelligent Contact in the Solar System, by Joan d'Arc.  Believers in extraterrestrial intelligent life (ETI) have no doubt been confronted with the few standard arguments covered in this book that are pitched by most skeptics. But are they logical and internally consistent? Or are they based on mistaken assumptions, government-media hogwash, and outmoded scientific concepts? Even skeptics may want to explore the logical grounds upon which their staunch protest against the existence of ETI is founded. Can Darwinian evolution actually prove we are alone in the Universe? This book illustrates that Darwinian evolution is actually not an empirically predictable or testable scientific paradigm. Darwinian evolution is a circular argument which serves to keep Earth humans earthbound. The Space Travel Argument Against the Existence of ETI will be shown to be dependent on three factors: (1) the persistent imposition of Earth-centered technological constraints (specifically, rocket technology and radio signals) implying an anthropocentric "you can't get here from there" attitude; (2) mathematical logic deduced from the faulty linear notions of Darwinian evolution, which only serve to put the "cart before the horse"; and (3) a circular and untestable hypothesis which essentially states "they aren't here because they aren't here." This book also shows that ancient anthropomorphic artifacts on Mars and the Moon are evidence of "Game Wardens" in our own solar system. Could the Earth be a controlled DNA repository for the ongoing creation and dissemination of life forms, including humans. **ISBN 1-58509-127-8 • 208 pages • 6 x 9 • trade paper • illustrated • $18.95**

104

Triumph of the Human Spirit: The Greatest Achievements of the Human Soul and How Its Power Can Change Your Life, by Paul Tice.  A triumph of the human spirit happens when we know we are right about something, put our heart into achieving its goal, and then succeed. There is no better feeling. People throughout history have triumphed while fighting for the highest ideal of all -- spiritual truth. Tice brings you back to relive and explore history's most incredible spiritual moments, bringing you into the lives of visionaries and great leaders who were in touch with their souls and followed their hearts. They explored God in their own way, exposed corruption and false teachings, or freed themselves and others from suppression. People like Gandhi, Joan of Arc, and Dr. King expressed exactly what they believed and changed the entire course of history. They were eliminated through violence, but on a spiritual level achieved victory because of their strong moral cause. Their spirit lives on, and the world was greatly improved. Tice covers other movements and people who may have physically failed, but spiritually triumphed. This book not only documents the history of spiritual giants, it shows how you can achieve your own spiritual triumph. In today's world we are free to explore the truth without fear of being tortured or executed. As a result, the rewards are great. Various exercises will strengthen the soul and reveal its hidden power. One can discover their true spiritual source with this work and will be able to tap into it. This is the perfect book for all those who believe in spiritual freedom and have a passion for the truth. **ISBN 1-885395-57-4 · 295 pages · 6 x 9 · trade paper · illustrated · $19.95**

 *That Old Time Religion: The Story of Religious Foundations,* by **Jordan Maxwell and Paul Tice.** This book proves there is nothing new under the sun — including Christianity. It gives a complete rundown of the stellar, lunar, and solar evolution of our religious systems; contains new, long-awaited, exhaustive research on the gods and our beliefs; includes research by Dr. Alan A. Snow, famous Dead Sea Scrolls scholar, on astrology in the Dead Sea Scrolls. Dr. Snow has been referred to by Sydney Ohmarr as the "world's greatest authority on astrology and the Dead Sea Scrolls." Includes 3 chapters by Paul Tice, a well known Gnostic minister. This book is illustrated, organized, and very comprehensible. Educate yourself with clear documented proof, and be prepared to have your belief system shattered! **ISBN 1-58509-100-6 · 220 pages · 6 x 9 · trade paper · $19.95**

Jumpin' Jehovah: Exposing the Atrocities of the Old Testament God, by **Paul Tice.** Was Jehovah a criminal? Was he psychotic? In the realm of the gods, was Jehovah just a renegade punk gone wild? Paul Tice has collected all the dirt on this shady historical character. Once you read this book, your views on God will never be the same again.  Jehovah is stripped bare of all his fabricated "godliness" and we discover in this book an entity with no sense of ethics, forgiveness or compassion. Jehovah delighted in roasting people alive and tormenting his followers in a variety of creative ways. Tice takes us from the very beginning, when this crafty character first came on the scene, and shows us how he conned and bullied his way to the top of the godly heap. Jehovah then maintained his standing through threats and coercion— and when that didn't work, he did what any mentally deranged god would do: he just moved in and killed people. Basic theological questions are explored like: Was Jehovah really a god, or a demon? Why did Jehovah never promise a heaven or any kind of reward to his followers? Does any entity who murders thousands of devoted followers deserve to be worshipped? What are the differences between a false god and a true one? Jehovah has stopped punishing people in terrible ways, so it's probably safe to buy this book. **ISBN 1-58509-102-2 · 104 pages · 6 x 9 · trade paper · $12.95**

Of Heaven and Earth: Essays Presented at the First Sitchin Studies Day, edited by Zecharia Sitchin. ISBN 1-885395-17-5 • 164 pages • 5 1/2 x 8 1/2 • trade paper • illustrated • $14.95

God Games: What Do You Do Forever?, by Neil Freer. ISBN 1-885395-39-6 • 312 pages • 6 x 9 • trade paper • $19.95

Space Travelers and the Genesis of the Human Form: Evidence of Intelligent Contact in the Solar System, by Joan d'Arc. ISBN 1-58509-127-8 • 208 pages • 6 x 9 • trade paper • illustrated • $18.95

Humanity's Extraterrestrial Origins: ET Influences on Humankind's Biological and Cultural Evolution, by Dr. Arthur David Horn with Lynette Mallory-Horn. ISBN 3-931652-31-9 • 373 pages • 6 x 9 • trade paper • $17.00

Past Shock: The Origin of Religion and Its Impact on the Human Soul, by Jack Barranger. ISBN 1-885395-08-6 • 126 pages • 6 x 9 • trade paper • illustrated • $12.95

Flying Serpents and Dragons: The Story of Mankind's Reptilian Past, by R.A. Boulay. ISBN 1-885395-38-8 • 276 pages • 6 x 9 • trade paper • illustrated • $19.95

Triumph of the Human Spirit: The Greatest Achievements of the Human Soul and How Its Power Can Change Your Life, by Paul Tice. ISBN 1-885395-57-4 • 295 pages • 6 x 9 • trade paper • illustrated • $19.95

Mysteries Explored: The Search for Human Origins, UFOs, and Religious Beginnings, by Jack Barranger and Paul Tice. ISBN 1-58509-101-4 • 104 pages • 6 x 9 • trade paper • $12.95

Mushrooms and Mankind: The Impact of Mushrooms on Human Consciousness and Religion, by James Arthur. ISBN 1-58509-151-0 • 180 pages • 6 x 9 • trade paper • $16.95

Vril or Vital Magnetism, with an Introduction by Paul Tice. ISBN 1-58509-030-1 • 124 pages • 5 1/2 x 8 1/2 • trade paper • $12.95

The Odic Force: Letters on Od and Magnetism, by Karl von Reichenbach. ISBN 1-58509-001-8 • 192 pages • 6 x 9 • trade paper • $15.95

The New Revelation: The Coming of a New Spiritual Paradigm, by Arthur Conan Doyle. ISBN 1-58509-220-7 • 124 pages • 6 x 9 • trade paper • $12.95

The Astral World: Its Scenes, Dwellers, and Phenomena, by Swami Panchadasi. ISBN 1-58509-071-9 • 104 pages • 6 x 9 • trade paper • $11.95

Reason and Belief: The Impact of Scientific Discovery on Religious and Spiritual Faith, by Sir Oliver Lodge. ISBN 1-58509-226-6 • 180 pages • 6 x 9 • trade paper • $17.95

William Blake: A Biography, by Basil De Selincourt. ISBN 1-58509-225-8 • 384 pages • 6 x 9 • trade paper • $28.95

The Divine Pymander: And Other Writings of Hermes Trismegistus, translated by John D. Chambers. ISBN 1-58509-046-8 • 196 pages • 6 x 9 • trade paper • $16.95

Theosophy and The Secret Doctrine, by Harriet L. Henderson. Includes **H.P. Blavatsky: An Outline of Her Life,** by Herbert Whyte, ISBN 1-58509-075-1 • 132 pages • 6 x 9 • trade paper • $13.95

The Light of Egypt, Volume One: The Science of the Soul and the Stars, by Thomas H. Burgoyne. ISBN 1-58509-051-4 • 320 pages • 6 x 9 • trade paper • illustrated • $24.95

The Light of Egypt, Volume Two: The Science of the Soul and the Stars, by Thomas H. Burgoyne. ISBN 1-58509-052-2 • 224 pages • 6 x 9 • trade paper • illustrated • $17.95

The Jumping Frog and 18 Other Stories: 19 Unforgettable Mark Twain Stories, by Mark Twain. ISBN 1-58509-200-2 • 128 pages • 6 x 9 • trade paper • $12.95

The Devil's Dictionary: A Guidebook for Cynics, by Ambrose Bierce. ISBN 1-58509-016-6 • 144 pages • 6 x 9 • trade paper • $12.95

The Smoky God: Or The Voyage to the Inner World, by Willis George Emerson. ISBN 1-58509-067-0 • 184 pages • 6 x 9 • trade paper • illustrated • $15.95

A Short History of the World, by H.G. Wells. ISBN 1-58509-211-8 • 320 pages • 6 x 9 • trade paper • $24.95

The Voyages and Discoveries of the Companions of Columbus, by Washington Irving. ISBN 1-58509-500-1 • 352 pages • 6 x 9 • hard cover • $39.95

History of Baalbek, by Michel Alouf. ISBN 1-58509-063-8 • 196 pages • 5 x 8 • trade paper • illustrated • $15.95

Ancient Egyptian Masonry: The Building Craft, by Sommers Clarke and R. Engelback. ISBN 1-58509-059-X • 350 pages • 6 x 9 • trade paper • illustrated • $26.95

That Old Time Religion: The Story of Religious Foundations, by Jordan Maxwell and Paul Tice. ISBN 1-58509-100-6 • 220 pages • 6 x 9 • trade paper • $19.95

Jumpin' Jehovah: Exposing the Atrocities of the Old Testament God, by Paul Tice. ISBN 1-58509-102-2 • 104 pages • 6 x 9 • trade paper • $12.95

The Book of Enoch: A Work of Visionary Revelation and Prophecy, Revealing Divine Secrets and Fantastic Information about Creation, Salvation, Heaven and Hell, translated by R. H. Charles. ISBN 1-58509-019-0 • 152 pages • 5 1/2 x 8 1/2 • trade paper • $13.95

The Book of Enoch: Translated from the Editor's Ethiopic Text and Edited with an Enlarged Introduction, Notes and Indexes, Together with a Reprint of the Greek Fragments, edited by R. H. Charles. ISBN 1-58509-080-8 • 448 pages • 6 x 9 • trade paper • $34.95

The Book of the Secrets of Enoch, translated from the Slavonic by W. R. Morfill. Edited, with Introduction and Notes by R. H. Charles. ISBN 1-58509-020-4 • 148 pages • 5 1/2 x 8 1/2 • trade paper • $13.95

Enuma Elish: The Seven Tablets of Creation, Volume One, by L. W. King. ISBN 1-58509-041-7 • 236 pages • 6 x 9 • trade paper • illustrated • $18.95

Enuma Elish: The Seven Tablets of Creation, Volume Two, by L. W. King. ISBN 1-58509-042-5 • 260 pages • 6 x 9 • trade paper • illustrated • $19.95

Enuma Elish, Volumes One and Two: The Seven Tablets of Creation, by L. W. King. Two volumes from above bound as one. ISBN 1-58509-043-3 • 496 pages • 6 x 9 • trade paper • illustrated • $38.90

The Archko Volume: Documents that Claim Proof to the Life, Death, and Resurrection of Christ, by Drs. McIntosh and Twyman. ISBN 1-58509-082-4 • 248 pages • 6 x 9 • trade paper • $20.95

The Lost Language of Symbolism: An Inquiry into the Origin of Certain Letters, Words, Names, Fairy-Tales, Folklore, and Mythologies, by Harold Bayley. ISBN 1-58509-070-0 • 384 pages • 6 x 9 • trade paper • $27.95

The Book of Jasher: A Suppressed Book that was Removed from the Bible, Referred to in Joshua and Second Samuel, translated by Albinus Alcuin (800 AD). ISBN 1-58509-081-6 • 304 pages • 6 x 9 • trade paper • $24.95

The Bible's Most Embarrassing Moments, with an Introduction by Paul Tice. ISBN 1-58509-025-5 • 172 pages • 5 x 8 • trade paper • $14.95

History of the Cross: The Pagan Origin and Idolatrous Adoption and Worship of the Image, by Henry Dana Ward. ISBN 1-58509-056-5 • 104 pages • 6 x 9 • trade paper • illustrated • $11.95

Was Jesus Influenced by Buddhism? A Comparative Study of the Lives and Thoughts of Gautama and Jesus, by Dwight Goddard. ISBN 1-58509-027-1 • 252 pages • 6 x 9 • trade paper • $19.95

History of the Christian Religion to the Year Two Hundred, by Charles B. Waite. ISBN 1-885395-15-9 • 556 pages. • 6 x 9 • hard cover • $25.00

Symbols, Sex, and the Stars, by Ernest Busenbark. ISBN 1-885395-19-1 • 396 pages • 5 1/2 x 8 1/2 • trade paper • $22.95

History of the First Council of Nice: A World's Christian Convention, A.D. 325, by Dean Dudley. ISBN 1-58509-023-9 • 132 pages • 5 1/2 x 8 1/2 • trade paper • $12.95

The World's Sixteen Crucified Saviors, by Kersey Graves. ISBN 1-58509-018-2 • 436 pages • 5 1/2 x 8 1/2 • trade paper • $29.95

Babylonian Influence on the Bible and Popular Beliefs: A Comparative Study of Genesis I.2, by A. Smythe Palmer. ISBN 1-58509-000-X • 124 pages • 6 x 9 • trade paper • $12.95

Biography of Satan: Exposing the Origins of the Devil, by Kersey Graves. ISBN 1-885395-11-6 • 168 pages • 5 1/2 x 8 1/2 • trade paper • $13.95

The Malleus Maleficarum: The Notorious Handbook Once Used to Condemn and Punish "Witches", by Heinrich Kramer and James Sprenger. ISBN 1-58509-098-0 • 332 pages • 6 x 9 • trade paper • $25.95

Crux Ansata: An Indictment of the Roman Catholic Church, by H. G. Wells. ISBN 1-58509-210-X • 160 pages • 6 x 9 • trade paper • $14.95

Emanuel Swedenborg: The Spiritual Columbus, by U.S.E. (William Spear). ISBN 1-58509-096-4 • 208 pages • 6 x 9 • trade paper • $17.95

Dragons and Dragon Lore, by Ernest Ingersoll. ISBN 1-58509-021-2 • 228 pages • 6 x 9 • trade paper • illustrated • $17.95

The Vision of God, by Nicholas of Cusa. ISBN 1-58509-004-2 • 160 pages • 5 x 8 • trade paper • $13.95

The Historical Jesus and the Mythical Christ: Separating Fact From Fiction, by Gerald Massey. ISBN 1-58509-073-5 • 244 pages • 6 x 9 • trade paper • $18.95

Gog and Magog: The Giants in Guildhall; Their Real and Legendary History, with an Account of Other Giants at Home and Abroad, by F.W. Fairholt. ISBN 1-58509-084-0 • 172 pages • 6 x 9 • trade paper • $16.95

The Origin and Evolution of Religion, by Albert Churchward. ISBN 1-58509-078-6 • 504 pages • 6 x 9 • trade paper • $39.95

The Origin of Biblical Traditions, by Albert T. Clay. ISBN 1-58509-065-4 • 220 pages • 5 1/2 x 8 1/2 • trade paper • $17.95

Aryan Sun Myths, by Sarah Elizabeth Titcomb, Introduction by Charles Morris. ISBN 1-58509-069-7 • 192 pages • 6 x 9 • trade paper • $15.95

The Social Record of Christianity, by Joseph McCabe. Includes *The Lies and Fallacies of the Encyclopedia Britannica,* ISBN 1-58509-215-0 • 204 pages • 6 x 9 • trade paper • $17.95

The History of the Christian Religion and Church During the First Three Centuries, by Dr. Augustus Neander. ISBN 1-58509-077-8 • 112 pages • 6 x 9 • trade paper • $12.95

Ancient Symbol Worship: Influence of the Phallic Idea in the Religions of Antiquity, by Hodder M. Westropp and C. Staniland Wake. ISBN 1-58509-048-4 • 120 pages • 6 x 9 • trade paper • illustrated • $12.95

The Gnosis: Or Ancient Wisdom in the Christian Scriptures, by William Kingsland. ISBN 1-58509-047-6 • 232 pages • 6 x 9 • trade paper • $18.95

The Evolution of the Idea of God: An Inquiry into the Origin of Religions, by Grant Allen. ISBN 1-58509-074-3 • 160 pages • 6 x 9 • trade paper • $14.95

107

Sun Lore of All Ages: A Survey of Solar Mythology, Folklore, Customs, Worship, Festivals, and Superstition, by William Tyler Olcott. ISBN 1-58509-044-1 • 316 pages • 6 x 9 • trade paper • $24.95

Nature Worship: An Account of Phallic Faiths and Practices Ancient and Modern, by the Author of Phallicism with an Introduction by Tedd St. Rain.ISBN 1-58509-049-2 • 112 pages • 6 x 9 • trade paper • illustrated • $12.95

Life and Religion, by Max Muller. ISBN 1-885395-10-8 • 237 pages • 5 1/2 x 8 1/2 • trade paper • $14.95

Jesus: God, Man, or Myth? An Examination of the Evidence, by Herbert Cutner. ISBN 1-58509-072-7 • 304 pages • 6 x 9 • trade paper • $23.95

Pagan and Christian Creeds: Their Origin and Meaning, by Edward Carpenter. ISBN 1-58509-024-7 • 316 pages • 5 1/2 x 8 1/2 • trade paper • $24.95

The Christ Myth: A Study, by Elizabeth Evans. ISBN 1-58509-037-9 • 136 pages • 6 x 9 • trade paper • $13.95

Popery: Foe of the Church and the Republic, by Joseph F. Van Dyke. ISBN 1-58509-058-1 • 336 pages • 6 x 9 • trade paper • illustrated • $25.95

Career of Religious Ideas, by Hudson Tuttle. ISBN 1-58509-066-2 • 172 pages • 5 x 8 • trade paper • $15.95

Buddhist Suttas: Major Scriptural Writings from Early Buddhism, by T.W. Rhys Davids.ISBN 1-58509-079-4 • 376 pages • 6 x 9 • trade paper • $27.95

Early Buddhism, by T. W. Rhys Davids. Includes *Buddhist Ethics: The Way to Salvation?,* by Paul Tice. ISBN 1-58509-076-X • 112 pages • 6 x 9 • trade paper • $12.95

The Fountain-Head of Religion: A Comparative Study of the Principal Religions of the World and a Manifestation of their Common Origin from the Vedas, by Ganga Prasad. ISBN 1-58509-054-9 • 276 pages • 6 x 9 • trade paper • $22.95

India: What Can It Teach Us?, by Max Muller. ISBN 1-58509-064-6 • 284 pages • 5 1/2 x 8 1/2 • trade paper • $22.95

Matrix of Power: How the World has Been Controlled by Powerful People Without Your Knowledge, by Jordan Maxwell. ISBN 1-58509-120-0 • 104 pages • 6 x 9 • trade paper • $12.95

Cyberculture Counterconspiracy: A Steamshovel Web Reader, Volume One, edited by Kenn Thomas. ISBN 1-58509-125-1 • 180 pages • 6 x 9 • trade paper • illustrated • $16.95

Cyberculture Counterconspiracy: A Steamshovel Web Reader, Volume Two, edited by Kenn Thomas. ISBN 1-58509-126-X • 132 pages • 6 x 9 • trade paper • illustrated • $13.95

Oklahoma City Bombing: The Suppressed Truth, by Jon Rappoport. ISBN 1-885395-22-1 • 112 pages • 5 1/2 x 8 1/2 • trade paper • $12.95

The Protocols of the Learned Elders of Zion, by Victor Marsden. ISBN 1-58509-015-8 • 312 pages • 6 x 9 • trade paper • $24.95

Secret Societies and Subversive Movements, by Nesta H. Webster. ISBN 1-58509-092-1 • 432 pages • 6 x 9 • trade paper • $29.95

The Secret Doctrine of the Rosicrucians, by Magus Incognito. ISBN 1-58509-091-3 • 256 pages • 6 x 9 • trade paper • $20.95

The Origin and Evolution of Freemasonry: Connected with the Origin and Evolution of the Human Race, by Albert Churchward.ISBN 1-58509-029-8 • 240 pages • 6 x 9 • trade paper • $18.95

The Lost Key: An Explanation and Application of Masonic Symbols, by Prentiss Tucker. ISBN 1-58509-050-6 • 192 pages • 6 x 9 • trade paper • illustrated • $15.95

The Character, Claims, and Practical Workings of Freemasonry, by Rev. C.G. Finney. ISBN 1-58509-094-8 • 288 pages • 6 x 9 • trade paper • $22.95

The Secret World Government or "The Hidden Hand": The Unrevealed in History, by Maj.-Gen., Count Cherep-Spiridovich. ISBN 1-58509-093-X • 270 pages • 6 x 9 • trade paper • $21.95

The Magus, Book One: A Complete System of Occult Philosophy, by Francis Barrett. ISBN 1-58509-031-X • 200 pages • 6 x 9 • trade paper • illustrated • $16.95

The Magus, Book Two: A Complete System of Occult Philosophy, by Francis Barrett. ISBN 1-58509-032-8 • 220 pages • 6 x 9 • trade paper • illustrated • $17.95

The Magus, Book One and Two: A Complete System of Occult Philosophy, by Francis Barrett. ISBN 1-58509-033-6 • 420 pages • 6 x 9 • trade paper • illustrated • $34.90

The Key of Solomon The King, by S. Liddell MacGregor Mathers. ISBN 1-58509-022-0 • 152 pages • 6 x 9 • trade paper • illustrated • $12.95

Magic and Mystery in Tibet, by Alexandra David-Neel. ISBN 1-58509-097-2 • 352 pages • 6 x 9 • trade paper • $26.95

The Comte de St. Germain, by I. Cooper Oakley. ISBN 1-58509-068-9 • 280 pages • 6 x 9 • trade paper • illustrated • $22.95

Alchemy Rediscovered and Restored, by A. Cockren. ISBN 1-58509-028-X • 156 pages • 5 1/2 x 8 1/2 • trade paper • $13.95

The 6th and 7th Books of Moses, with an Introduction by Paul Tice. ISBN 1-58509-045-X • 188 pages • 6 x 9 • trade paper • illustrated • $16.95

CPSIA information can be obtained
at www.ICGtesting.com
Printed in the USA
BVHW030232290120
570801BV00001B/17

9 781585 091010